Microsoft® Office Access® 2010: Part 1

Microsoft® Office Access® 2010: Part 1

Part Number: 091001
Course Edition: 2.2

Acknowledgements

PROJECT TEAM

Author	Media Designer	Content Editor
Brian S. Wilson	Alex Tong	Tricia Murphy

Notices

DISCLAIMER

TRADEMARK NOTICES

Microsoft® Office Access® 2010: Part 1

About This Course

Data is everywhere. Whether you are at the grocery store, office, laboratory, classroom, or ball park, you are awash in data: prices, schedules, performance measures, lab results, recipes, contact information, quality metrics, market indices, grades, and statistics.

Most job roles today involve some form of *data management*. In the case of data workers, it may be their primary job task. For some, like research scientists and accountants, data management may be a strong component of the job. And for others, such as sales clerks or those in the skilled trades, data management may consist of an incidental job responsibility such as time reporting or recording a sale. But virtually everyone is affected in some way by the need to manage data.

A relational database application such as Microsoft® Office Access® 2010 can help you and your organization collect and manage large amounts of data. Access is a versatile tool. You can use it as a personal data management tool (for your use alone), or you can use it as a construction set to develop applications for an entire department or organization. In this course, you will learn how to use Access 2010 to manage your data, including creating a new database, constructing tables, designing forms and reports, and creating queries to join, filter, and sort data.

You can also use this course to prepare for the Microsoft Office Specialist (MOS) Certification exam for Microsoft Access 2010.

Course Description

Target Student

This course is designed for students who wish to establish a foundational understanding of Microsoft Office Access 2010, including the skills necessary to create a new database, construct data tables, design forms and reports, and create queries.

Course Prerequisites

To ensure success, students should be familiar with using personal computers, and should have experience using a keyboard and mouse. Students should be comfortable in the Windows® 7 environment, and be able to use Windows 7 to manage information on their computers. Specific tasks the students should be able to perform include: launching and closing applications, navigating basic file structures, and managing files and folders. To meet this prerequisite, you can take any one or more of the following Logical Operations courses:

- *Microsoft® Windows® 7: Level 1*
- *Introduction to Personal Computers Using Windows® 7*

Course Objectives

In this course, you will learn to create and manage a fundamental Access 2010 database.

You will:

- Navigate within the Microsoft Access application environment and create a simple database.
- Organize and manage data stored within Access tables.
- Use queries to join, sort, and filter data from different tables.
- Create advanced queries, including action queries, parameter queries, PivotTables, and PivotCharts.
- Create and format custom reports.
- Customize Access configuration options.

The LogicalCHOICE Home Screen

http://www.lo-choice.com

The LogicalCHOICE Home screen is your entry point to the LogicalCHOICE learning experience, of which this course manual is only one part. Visit the LogicalCHOICE Course screen both during and after class to make use of the world of support and instructional resources that make up the LogicalCHOICE experience.

Log-on and access information for your LogicalCHOICE environment will be provided with your class experience. On the LogicalCHOICE Home screen, you can access the LogicalCHOICE Course screens for your specific courses.

Each LogicalCHOICE Course screen will give you access to the following resources:

- eBook: an interactive electronic version of the printed book for your course.
- LearnTOs: brief animated components that enhance and extend the classroom learning experience.

Depending on the nature of your course and the choices of your learning provider, the LogicalCHOICE Course screen may also include access to elements such as:

- The interactive eBook.
- Social media resources that enable you to collaborate with others in the learning community using professional communications sites such as LinkedIn or microblogging tools such as Twitter.
- Checklists with useful post-class reference information.
- Any course files you will download.
- The course assessment.
- Notices from the LogicalCHOICE administrator.
- Virtual labs, for remote access to the technical environment for your course.
- Your personal whiteboard for sketches and notes.
- Newsletters and other communications from your learning provider.
- Mentoring services.
- A link to the website of your training provider.
- The LogicalCHOICE store.

Visit your LogicalCHOICE Home screen often to connect, communicate, and extend your learning experience!

How to Use This Book

As You Learn

This book is divided into lessons and topics, covering a subject or a set of related subjects. In most cases, lessons are arranged in order of increasing proficiency.

The results-oriented topics include relevant and supporting information you need to master the content. Each topic has various types of activities designed to enable you to practice the guidelines and procedures as well as to solidify your understanding of the informational material presented in the course. Procedures and guidelines are presented in a concise fashion along with activities and discussions. Information is provided for reference and reflection in such a way as to facilitate understanding and practice.

Data files for various activities as well as other supporting files for the course are available by download from the LogicalCHOICE Course screen. In addition to sample data for the course exercises, the course files may contain media components to enhance your learning and additional reference materials for use both during and after the course.

At the back of the book, you will find a glossary of the definitions of the terms and concepts used throughout the course. You will also find an index to assist in locating information within the instructional components of the book.

As You Review

Any method of instruction is only as effective as the time and effort you, the student, are willing to invest in it. In addition, some of the information that you learn in class may not be important to you immediately, but it may become important later. For this reason, we encourage you to spend some time reviewing the content of the course after your time in the classroom.

As a Reference

The organization and layout of this book make it an easy-to-use resource for future reference. Taking advantage of the glossary, index, and table of contents, you can use this book as a first source of definitions, background information, and summaries.

Course Icons

Watch throughout the material for these visual cues:

Icon	Description
	A **Note** provides additional information, guidance, or hints about a topic or task.
	A **Caution** helps make you aware of places where you need to be particularly careful with your actions, settings, or decisions so that you can be sure to get the desired results of an activity or task.
	LearnTO notes show you where an associated LearnTO is particularly relevant to the content. Access LearnTOs from your LogicalCHOICE Course screen.
	Checklists provide job aids you can use after class as a reference to performing skills back on the job. Access checklists from your LogicalCHOICE Course screen.
	Social notes remind you to check your LogicalCHOICE Course screen for opportunities to interact with the LogicalCHOICE community using social media.
	Notes Pages are intentionally left blank for you to write on.

1 | Getting Started with Access

Lesson Time: 1 hour, 30 minutes

Lesson Objectives

In this lesson, you will get started with Access. You will:

- Navigate within the Microsoft Access application environment.

- Create an Access database.

- Use Access Help to find documentation on a specific Access feature.

Lesson Introduction

Access enables you to build your own tools for collecting, analyzing, and reporting on data. Like the other Microsoft® Office suite applications, Access is versatile and can be used in many different ways. In this lesson, you will learn what Access can do by systematically analyzing and using an existing Access database. You will explore potential uses for Access. You will develop your own database from scratch, and you will use the Help system to get acquainted with features of the Access application environment.

TOPIC A

Orientation to Microsoft Access

Microsoft® Office Access® 2010 provides tools that you can use to structure and organize your data. The first step in mastering Access is to get comfortable working with the Access user interface.

Microsoft Access 2010

Access is an application that enables you to create and manage a database. A *database* is a collection of data that is organized so you can efficiently store, retrieve, analyze, and present *information*. Data in a database typically models or records real-world information. You might use a database to store records of assets or inventory, customer information, sales transactions, maintenance schedules, statistical data, quality measures, and so forth. In fact, virtually any sort of information that can be entered into a computer can be stored in a database.

Why Use a Database Application?

You might think of *data* as a precursor to *knowledge*. Without any organization to it, raw data is not especially useful. But once data has been meaningfully structured and organized, as in a database application, it emerges as information; that is, something that informs. Likewise, when information is further analyzed and processed into a model that can be applied in a useful way, it becomes knowledge. Consider how beneficial it might be for an organization to reveal the following information.

Data	Information	Knowledge
Dept1=7.5, Dept2=3.2, Dept3=4.5, ...	Which department produces the most defects	Where and how defects can be reduced
Site1=0, Site2=1, Site3=7, Site4=0, ...	Which street intersections are the site of the largest number of accidents	Steps that can be taken to reduce accidents
Prod1=$34,500, Prod2=$15,210, Prod3=$7,102, Prod4=$3,511, Prod5=$34,500, ...	Which product lines bring in the most revenue and which bring in the least	How to restructure our product lines to increase profits

Knowledge supports good decision-making within an organization.

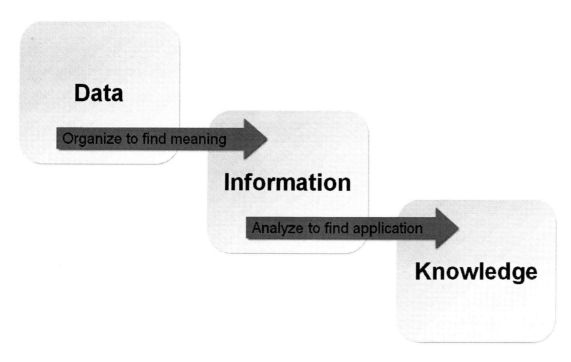

Figure 1-1: Transform data into knowledge.

Why Use Access as Your Database Application?

If you have Access on your computer, you likely also have Microsoft® Excel®. Although Excel is generally geared more toward working with numbers than mixed data (numbers *and* text, for example), many people use Excel for data management tasks. Excel can handle some database tasks such as *filtering*, *sorting*, searching, and reporting. Conversely, Access can be used for tasks that are traditionally in the realm of spreadsheet programs, such as accounting tasks, analytics, and charting. It's not surprising that Excel and Access share capabilities, as they have been part of the same software suite for many years and have been designed to work well together. Since Access is part of the Microsoft® Office suite, deciding whether to use Access or Excel does not have to be an either/or decision. You can use the tools in combination, and many users do just that.

You might choose Access over Excel for specific database management tasks because Access:

- Is optimized for database management. It generally performs faster and can support larger sets of data than Excel.
- Is designed to manage complex relationships between separate lists (or tables) of data than Excel.
- Provides better support for data input validation (enforcing correct form or values of data) than Excel.
- Is generally better suited to work with mixed data (data that is not primarily numeric) than Excel.
- Provides extensive support for report generation.
- Can support multiple user databases.
- Provides good integration for use as a front-end development tool for enterprise databases such as Microsoft SQL Server® and Oracle.

Access and Enterprise Database Management Systems

Likewise, it may not always be clear whether you should use Access, which is primarily a desktop application, or an enterprise database management system, such as Microsoft SQL Server or Oracle.

You may choose to use Access instead of another database development tool because Access is:

- Widely used. There are many resources and developer communities to help you.
- Relatively inexpensive. In fact, you may already have it on your computer.

- A much smaller startup investment. Access is relatively easy to install and configure, and it may provide an easier path into database development than other tools geared primarily toward programmers.
- Scalable. You can use Access alone until your needs outgrow it. Then you can use it in conjunction with an enterprise database. Microsoft provides tools to facilitate moving from a standalone Access database to SQL Server.

Again, whether to use Access or an enterprise database is not an either/or decision. You can use Microsoft Access with an enterprise database server to create a solution that will scale to hundreds or more users. If you create a database in Access for a small user audience and then find that the number of users grows over time, it is possible to upsize from Access to a larger database application such as Microsoft SQL Server. In fact, Access is often used to quickly create an application front-end (what the user interacts directly with) for a powerful database back-end such as Oracle or SQL Server.

Access as a Web Development Tool

Access can also be used as a web development tool. There are many ways to publish Access database data to the web, as simply as exporting a PDF report or static Hypertext Markup Language (HTML) web page and as complex as developing a web services application that pulls data from an Access database when requested by users and providing that data in formats that include HTML, Extensible Markup Language (XML), or some other web format. With the Office 2010 version, Access gained the ability to publish dynamic web applications directly to a SharePoint® server. Databases published this way contain live data from the current version of data in the database. Users do not have to view data that started becoming stale the moment it was published to a static HTML or PDF page.

Objects in Access Databases

Access uses six different objects in the creation and modification of databases:

- **Tables** store data in rows and columns.
- **Forms** provide a graphical interface for modifying data in tables.
- **Queries** transform data in tables, such as sorting a table by certain parameters.
- **Reports** provide a streamlined way of viewing data.
- **Macros** allow you to automate tasks within a database.
- **Modules** are similar to macros, but are written in the Visual Basic for Applications (VBA) programming language.

 Note: Macros and modules are not covered until Part 3 of this Access 2010 series of courses.

ACTIVITY 1–1
Considering Potential Uses for Access

Scenario

Consider the following questions.

1. Why did you decide to use Access?

2. Considering the work you do, what sorts of tools or databases would you like to create in Access?

3. Regarding your response to the previous question, what data might you need to keep within such a database?

Access Files

Access 2010 databases are stored in files, similar to the way that Microsoft® Word and Microsoft® Excel® documents are stored in files. Access 2010 database files have the .accdb file-name extension. When you save a database file, if you do not provide the .accdb file-name extension, Access adds it for you. A single Access database file may hold up to 2 gigabytes (GB) of data, with up to 32,768 unique objects. Up to 255 users can access data from a single Access database file at the same time.

Saving

As you enter data, Access automatically saves your changes as you move to another record. However, when you change the design of tables, queries, forms, and other objects, you need to save those changes by selecting **File→Save**. Of course, if you aren't sure that your data has been saved, you can issue the **Save** command to be sure.

Enable Content

Because Access databases may contain active content (scripts and other executable code), you should verify that the Access content you are viewing came from a trusted source. By default, Access is configured to prompt you to confirm that the database you opened is from a source that you trust. If you are opening a file from a trusted source, select **Enable Content** when you are prompted.

 Access the Checklist tile on your LogicalCHOICE course screen for reference information and job aids on How to Open a Database

ACTIVITY 1-2
Launching Access and Opening a Database

Data Files

C:\091001Data\Getting Started with Access\Inventory Database.accdb

Scenario

Woodworker's Wheelhouse was founded in 1955 as W.B. Spall Lumber Company, a small family-run home improvement (lumber and hardware) store in suburban Greene City until 1998, when the last of the Spall family retired. That year, the company was sold, and the new owner began transforming it into a web-based business, focusing on selling hardwood lumber, tools, and other supplies for woodworkers and other hobbyists. While the web business grows, a bricks-and-mortar storefront is still maintained, and a small selection of home improvement supplies are still sold, both locally and over the web. Eventually, the home improvement items will be phased out.

You are the web and database developer for Woodworker's Wheelhouse. To replace the current inventory system (the same pencil-and-paper system the company used in the 1950s), you have begun creating an inventory database in Microsoft Access 2010. Some of the database structure has already been created and some entries have already been entered into inventory. You need to make some changes to information within the database. To do so, you will launch Access and open the database.

---

1. Launch Microsoft Access. With no database open, the **File** tab is already shown for you, so you can select an existing database or create a new one.

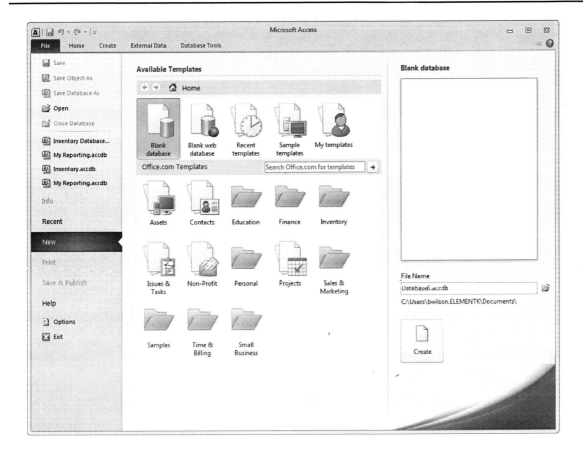

2. Select **Open**.

3. Navigate to the C:\091001Data\Getting Started with Access directory and select the **Inventory Database.accdb** database file.

4. Select **Open**.

5. Observe the Access application window. The title bar shows that the Inventory Database database is loaded, but the document area is blank.

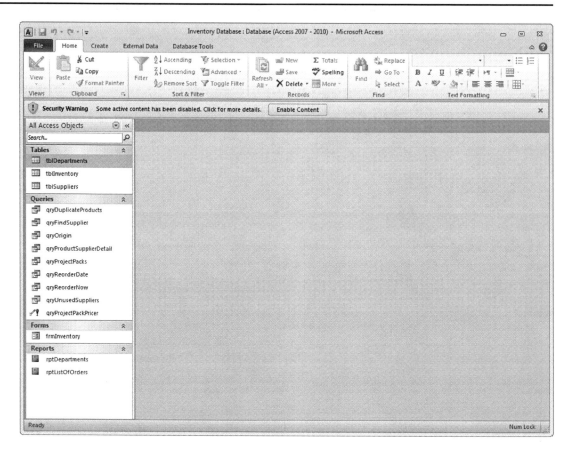

6. If you see the security warning, select **Enable Content**.

The Access 2010 Application Window

The Access 2010 application window displays application features that enable you to create, enhance, and manage Access databases. The application provides features to input, store, and output data, and enables you to import and export data from and to external applications. The application window also provides you with access to the integrated Help feature, which provides instructive support on using Access.

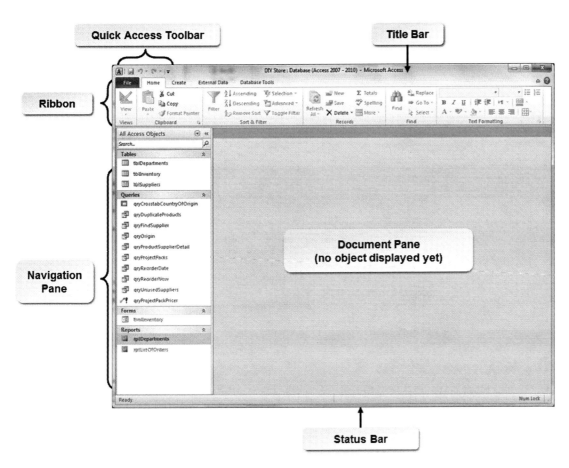

Figure 1-2: Access 2010 window components.

Component	Description
Navigation pane	List on the left side of the application window, which displays objects in the database, including tables, queries, forms, and reports.
Quick Access Toolbar	Small button panel at the top-left corner of the application window, which contains commonly used commands. You can customize this toolbar to include other commands.
The ribbon	This graphical menu panel, common to all Microsoft Office applications, contains commands which are organized into tabs and groups.
Status bar	The bottom panel of the application window displays information about the application and currently selected database object, and provides options for viewing the currently selected database object.
Title bar	A caption at the top of the application window displays the name of the open database.

Tabbed Document Windows

When you open database objects such as tables, queries, and forms, Access displays them as tabbed sub-documents within the document pane. You can have multiple objects open at the same time, and can move among them by selecting the object's tab. When you right-click the tab, Access provides a convenient shortcut menu with commonly used commands that pertain to the type of object contained within that tab.

Tables

A table is a storage container that stores related data in rows and columns. Rows display information about each item in the table. Columns display categories in the table. A table has a header row with a descriptor for each column.

Tables contain various components that can be individually accessed and manipulated.

Table Element	Description
Record	A row of a table data, which contains a complete set of data for a single entity. For example, a record might contain all related information for a business contact, including their name, address, phone number, and so forth.
Field	A column of table data, which contains a single data element within a record. For example, a record meant to hold data about a rectangle might hold three fields: height, width, and the rectangle's unique ID.
Value	A single data value held within a field.

Flat vs. Relational Databases

There are two types of databases with respect to tables: *flat databases* and *relational databases*. Flat databases contain a single table of data, while relational databases contain multiple tables of data that relate to each other through certain key fields. Relational databases are more flexible and streamlined. If, for example, your database contains only a single table of orders placed for your business, then finding or changing specific information about a customer might be difficult, especially if that customer is listed more than once in the orders table. With a relational database, there would be separate tables for both orders and customers. This would help increase your ability to use and change information in your database. The main advantage of flat databases are that they are easier to implement and to maintain. Not all situations would benefit from the added complexity of multiple tables.

 Access the Checklist tile on your LogicalCHOICE course screen for reference information and job aids on How to Navigate and Edit in a Table

ACTIVITY 1-3
Navigating and Editing Data in Tables

Before You Begin

You have opened the database C:\091001Data\Getting Started with Access\Inventory Database.accdb. No database objects are yet open in the document pane.

Scenario

You are the database developer for a small lumber and hardware store that is reinventing itself as a web store for do-it-yourselfers and woodworking hobbyists. You are moving the company's record-keeping from paper records to a database. You have started developing a product database to track inventory and to hold information regarding your suppliers. You need to delete one product from the database and change the supplier information for another. You have already opened the database, but you do not yet have a view into the data.

---

1. View the contents of a data table.

    a) Observe the navigation pane. Various types of database objects—tables, queries, forms, and reports—are listed. They have been named to help you know what type of object they are. For example, tblInventory (pronounced "table inventory") begins with "tbl" so you know it is a table.

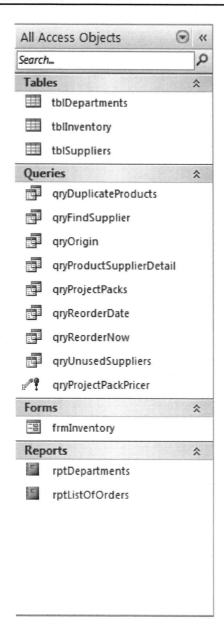

b) In the navigation pane, double-click **tblInventory**. A datasheet appears, in which you can view and edit the contents of the table.

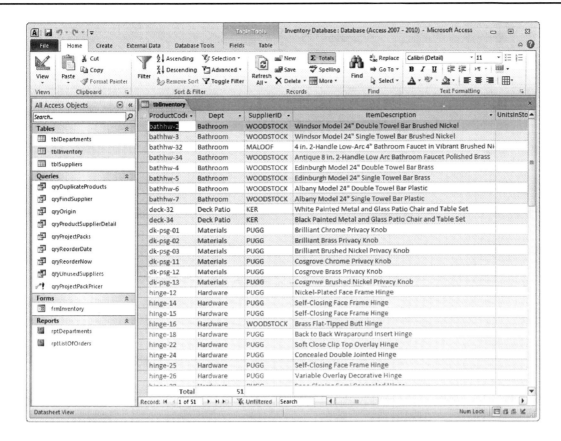

c) Observe the datasheet for tblInventory. Note the following:

- A record of data for a specific product is contained within a single row.
- A field is contained within a single column. For example, the first column contains the **ProductCode** field. Each column contains one type of information.
- A value is the actual data stored for a particular field and record. For example, the **SupplierID** field for the deck-32 record contains the value "KER."

2. Save a copy of the database.

> **Note:** This course uses a streamlined notation for ribbon commands. They'll appear as "[Ribbon Tab]→[Group]→[Button or Control]" as in "select Home→Clipboard→Paste." If the group name isn't needed for navigation or there isn't a group, it's omitted, as in "select **File→Open.**"

a) Select **File→Save Database As**. In the **Microsoft Access** message box, select **Yes** to have Access close the open object. The **Save As** dialog box is shown.
b) Browse to the C:\091001Data\Getting Started with Access folder.
c) Change the file name to *My Updated Database* and select **Save**. The .accdb file-name extension will be added automatically. Since this is a new file that you have not opened before, you may be shown a security prompt.
d) If you have been prompted with a security warning, select **Enable Content**.

3. Delete a record.

a) Open **tblInventory** by double-clicking it in the navigation pane.
b) Use the scroll bar to scroll down until you see the record with the **ProductCode** win-dbl-3000. You will no longer carry this product in your store, so you will delete it from the database.
c) Select the box on the left side of the win-dbl-3000 row to select the entire row (record).

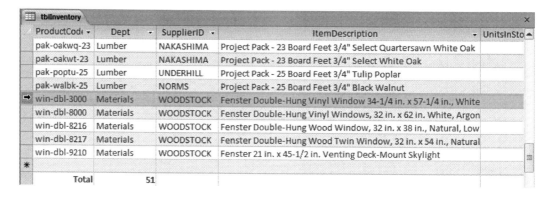

d) Select **Home→Records→Delete**.

You are prompted to confirm deletion.

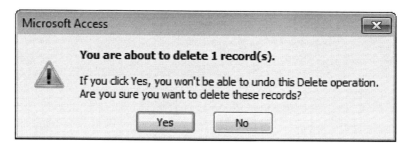

e) Select **Yes**.

f) Observe that the win-dbl-3000 record has been deleted.

4. Change the **ItemDescription** for the bathhw-2 product.

a) Scroll to view the top row of the datasheet.

b) Select the box where the bathhw-2 row and the **ItemDescription** column intersect. The current value for this record is "Windsor Model 24" Double Towel Bar Brushed Nickel."

c) Drag to highlight all the text in the **ItemDescription** field.

d) Type *Gotham Model 24" Double Towel Bar Stainless*

5. Add a new record to the tblInventory table.

a) Scroll to the bottom of the tblInventory table and observe the record with a * in the left column of the tblInventory table. Think of this row as being *the last record plus one*. It is a new, blank record that provides a ready means to add a new record.

b) Select the first field (ProductCode) of the * row to select the field for data entry.

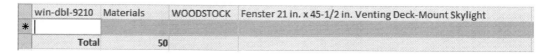

c) Type *hw-1* and press **Enter**. The value is entered, and the next field is selected.

d) Enter the following values to fill in the rest of your new record.

Field	Value
Dept	Materials
SupplierID	WOODSTOCK
ItemDescription	Bolt, Hex Head Stainless 1/4-20 x 3"
UnitsInStock	50
TargetInventory	50
ReorderLevel	25
LastOrdered	2012-06-01
Location	Showroom
Rack	4
Origin	Canada
OurUnitCost	.18
RetailPrice	.25

e) Select **File→Save** to save the database.

6. Right-click the **tblInventory** tab and select **Close** to close the table.

Forms

Forms provide a graphical user interface (GUI) for entering and modifying table data. Forms do not actually contain data. They simply provide a view into table data. Forms are typically designed to facilitate repetitive data entry tasks.

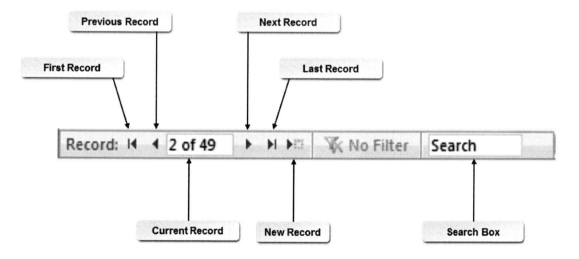

Figure 1-3: The Record navigation bar.

The *Record navigation bar* provides controls that you can use to navigate among records.

 Access the Checklist tile on your LogicalCHOICE course screen for reference information and job aids on How to Navigate and Edit in a Form

ACTIVITY 1-4
Navigating and Editing Data in a Form

Before You Begin

You have made changes to the data in Inventory Database.accdb and saved them to My Updated Database.accdb. My Updated Database.accdb is open, and no database objects are opened in the document pane.

Scenario

As the database developer for Woodworker's Wheelhouse, you have used table datasheets to enter data, but you plan to hire some temporary workers to enter thousands of records into the database. You want to provide them something a bit more streamlined for data entry than datasheets. Forms provide the solution.

---

1. Open a form.
   a) In the navigation pane, double-click **frmInventory**. An entry form appears.

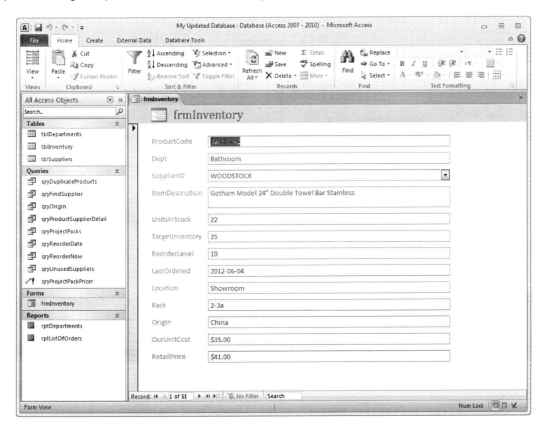

   b) Observe the form. In this form, you can view, enter, and modify data in the database. Various data entry controls are shown, along with labels identifying what information is contained within them. If you have many fields (columns), a form can be configured to minimize or avoid the need for horizontal and vertical scrolling as you work within a single record, which might be less tedious than working in a table's **Datasheet** view.

2. Navigate within the form view.

---

a) Observe the **Record** navigation bar. This portion of the screen provides navigation controls and indications. You can see that you are viewing record 1.

b) Select the controls on the **Record** navigation bar to try them out.

Navigation Bar Control	Function
Next Record button	Moves to the next record in the table.
Previous Record button	Moves to the previous record in the table.
Last Record button	Moves to the last record in the table. If you select **Next Record** after the last record, a new record will be shown.
First Record button	Moves to the first record in the table.
New Record button	Moves to the new record row. If you enter data, it will be saved in the new record.

c) Navigate to record 18. The **ProductCode** for this record is hinge-14.

d) Use your mouse to highlight the value in the **UnitsInStock** field.

e) Type *75* to change the selected value.

f) Press **Tab** to advance to the next text box. The value of **100** is already selected, so you could type to replace it if you wanted to.

g) Observe the fields in this form. Most are free text entry, but the SupplierID field is a drop-down list. As an Access database developer, you can determine which values entered in the database should be freeform text and which should picked from a list.

h) Click the drop-down box for the **SupplierID** field and observe the list.

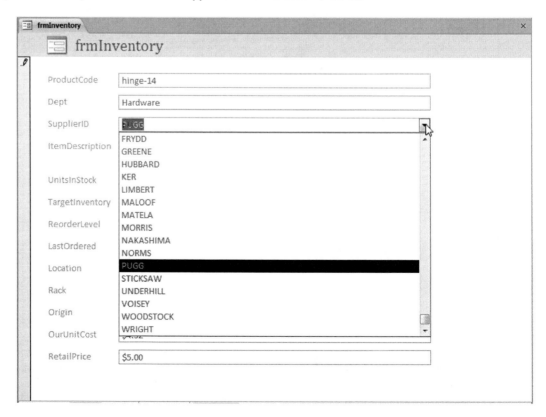

i) Select **WOODSTOCK**.

j) In the navigation pane, double-click **tblSuppliers**.

k) Observe the records in the tblSuppliers table. This table is the source of supplier IDs that were shown in the **SupplierID** drop-down list.

l) In upper-left corner of the Access application window, in the **Quick Access Toolbar**, select the **Save** button. . This is a shortcut for selecting **File→Save**.

m) Close the **tblSuppliers** tab.

n) Close the **frmInventory** tab.

Queries

While tables give a database its substance, that substance is lifeless until you breathe life into the database through the addition of queries. Queries transform table data. For example, a query can:

- Join data from multiple tables to produce a new, combined data set.
- Sort results by one or more fields.
- Filter results based on criteria.
- Prompt the user for additional criteria before producing output.
- Perform calculations, reorganize, and summarize data.
- Make mass updates to table data, such as copying or deleting records.

Because they can perform complex transformations and present table data from a completely different perspective, queries provide a powerful tool for data analysis and reporting.

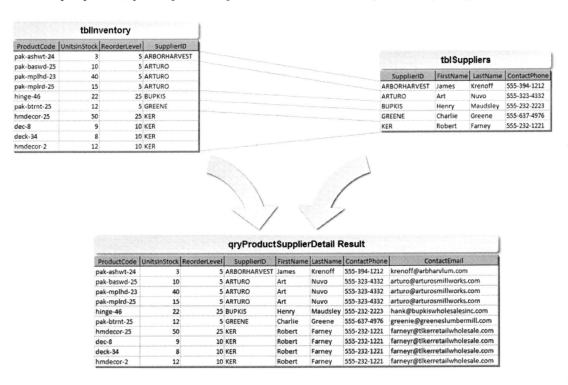

Figure 1–4: A query join.

Access the Checklist tile on your LogicalCHOICE course screen for reference information and job aids on How to Run a Query

ACTIVITY 1-5
Using Queries

Before You Begin

My Updated Database.accdb is open, and no database objects are opened in the document pane.

Scenario

You understand that there are design benefits to using multiple tables in your database. For example, it is not a good idea to duplicate supplier contact information in the record for each product that is provided by that supplier. If suppliers change their address or phone number, you would have to update that information in every record where it appears.

On the other hand, it would be very convenient to show contact information right next to the product—for example, when you are preparing to place an order. Fortunately, you can use a query to join data from multiple tables in a temporary view.

1. Use a query to show joined data from multiple tables.
   a) In the navigation pane, double-click **qryProductSupplierDetail**.

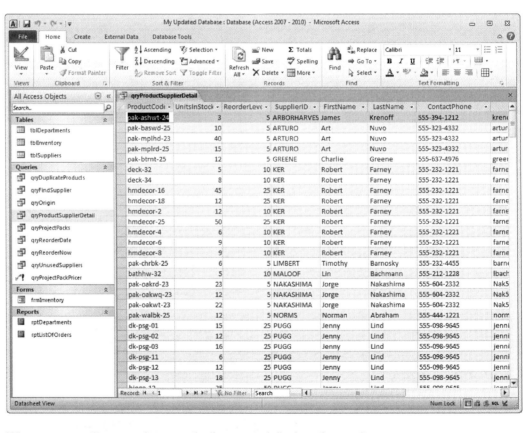

When you open the query, it automatically runs and displays the results.

   b) Observe the results of the query. The query results are presented like a single table, but in fact, this query *joins data from two tables* into a temporary view. Product information from tblInventory (**ProductCode**, **UnitsInStock**, and **ReorderLevel**) is shown along with related supplier contact information from tblSuppliers (**FirstName**, **LastName**, etc.). The **SupplierID** field exists in both tables and provides the link that enables the two tables to be joined in a query. Results are sorted by **SupplierID**.

c) Close qryProductSupplierDetail.

2. Use a query to filter data.

a) In the navigation pane, double-click **qryProjectPacks**. This query *filters data*. It is showing records from tblInventory, but has filtered the results to show only product codes that begin with **pak-**.

ProductCode	ItemDescription	UnitsInStock	ReorderLevel
pak-ashwt-24	Project Pack - 24 Board Feet 3/4" Select White Ash	3	5
pak-baswd-25	Project Pack - 25 Board Feet 3/4" Select Basswood	10	5
pak-btrnt-25	Project Pack - 25 Board Feet 3/4" Select Butternut	12	5
pak-chrbk-25	Project Pack - 25 Board Feet 3/4" Select Black Cherry	6	5
pak-mplhd-23	Project Pack - 23 Board Feet 3/4" Select Hard Maple	40	5
pak-mplrd-25	Project Pack - 25 Board Feet 3/4" Select Red Maple	15	5
pak-oakrd-23	Project Pack - 23 Board Feet 3/4" Select Red Oak	23	5
pak-oakwq-23	Project Pack - 23 Board Feet 3/4" Select Quartersawn White Oak	12	5
pak-oakwt-23	Project Pack - 23 Board Feet 3/4" Select White Oak	22	5
pak-poptu-25	Project Pack - 25 Board Feet 3/4" Tulip Poplar	23	5
pak-walbk-25	Project Pack - 25 Board Feet 3/4" Black Walnut	12	5

3. Use an action query that accepts an input parameter.

a) Scroll to the right to view the **RetailPrice** values for the project packs. You will run an action query to increase the price for all project packs.

RetailPrice
$107.71
$87.52
$125.66
$171.67
$117.81
$102.10
$109.96
$139.13
$109.96
$87.52
$170.54

b) Close qryProjectPacks.

c) In the navigation pane, double-click **qryProjectPackPricer**.

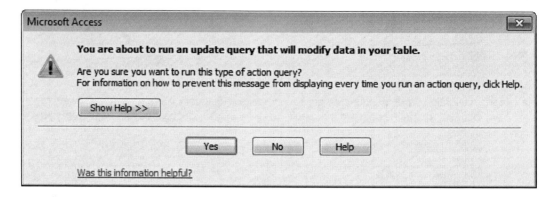

d) Select **Yes**.

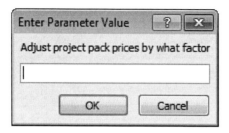

e) Type *1.25* and press **Enter**. You will raise the price of all project packs to 1.25 times the current price, or an increase of 25 percent.

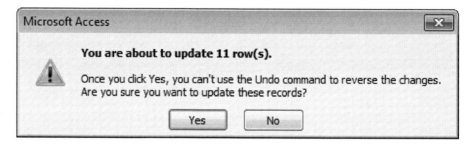

f) Select **Yes**.
g) In the navigation pane, double-click **qryProjectPacks**. Scroll to the right to view the new prices and compare them to the previous prices. The query has updated all project pack prices by the amount you specified.

Before	After
RetailPrice ▾	RetailPrice ▾
$107.71	$134.64
$87.52	$109.40
$125.66	$157.08
$171.67	$214.58
$117.81	$147.26
$102.10	$127.63
$109.96	$137.45
$139.13	$173.91
$109.96	$137.45
$87.52	$109.40
$170.54	$213.18

h) Close qryProjectPacks.

4. Save the database.

Reports

Reports provide a publish-ready view of data that you can output to various print or digital formats. You can design a report to include graphic and formatting elements such as images, fonts, and color themes. You can control the layout and use of white space to suit your needs. Reports can present table data directly, but they are often used to present data that has been sorted, filtered, and transformed through a query. Reports can be printed as a hard copy, or they can be exported to a Portable Document Format (PDF) for an easy-to-read electronic copy that preserves the original formatting.

 Access the Checklist tile on your LogicalCHOICE course screen for reference information and job aids on How to Run and Print Reports

ACTIVITY 1–6
Using Reports

Before You Begin

My Updated Database.accdb is open, and no database objects are opened in the document pane.

Scenario

Although computer databases can help reduce paper use, in some cases, a printout is necessary. Or you might need to publish a copy of the database to a web-friendly format that can be viewed but not modified by readers. Access' reporting features enable you to accomplish such tasks.

Now that you have updated the product database, you will prepare some reports from the current data.

---

1. Open rptListOfOrders.

2. Right-click the **rptListOfOrders** tab and select **Print Preview**. In **Print Preview**, the report is shown as it will appear when printed, and the navigation bar is added to the view so you can navigation between pages.

3. Observe the report. Reports are optimized for printing and presentation. Like forms, reports can have a freeform layout, or they can be organized in columns and rows like a table. Reports can include graphics, custom color themes, fonts, borders, and other visual elements.

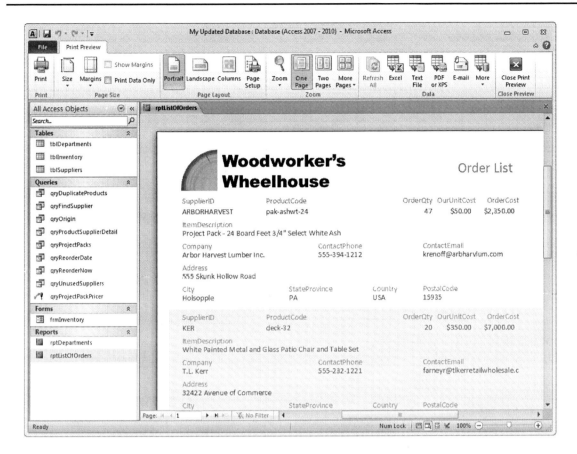

4. Use the navigation bar at the bottom of the view to browse other report pages.

5. Close rptListOfOrders.

The Ribbon

The ribbon is a graphical menu panel that appears at the top of the application window. Tabs are organized in groups related to the type of task being performed, and each tab is further divided into groups of related commands. You can customize the ribbon by adding, removing, or rearranging tabs, groups, and buttons. You can hide the ribbon to gain more working space in the document area by double-clicking any active tab.

Ribbon Tabs

Tabs divide the ribbon into groups of commands that relate to similar types of tasks. The ribbon is organized to keep navigation to a minimum. The following ribbon tabs are provided in Access 2010.

Tab	Commands
File	Open, save, publish, create, print, and close a database. Also displays recently opened files, enables you to view and edit database properties, and provides access to Help, Options, and exiting the application.
Home	Basic formatting and search options, as well as functional groups such as **Views**, **Sort & Filter**, and **Records**, that are oriented toward specific types of work you will perform in Access objects.
Create	Create new database objects, such as tables, queries, forms, and reports.

Tab	Commands
External Data	Enable you to move large amounts of data into and out of Access. A wide variety of data formats are supported, including Excel spreadsheets, text files, XML, and PDF.
Database Tools	Enable you to perform certain types of database-wide tasks.

 Note: If you want to know more about the Microsoft Office ribbon, view the LearnTO **Navigate the Office 2010 Ribbon** presentation from the **LearnTO** tile on the LogicalCHOICE Course screen.

Contextual Tabs

Contextual tabs are additional tabs displayed on the ribbon when you work with objects such as tables, forms, queries, or reports. The commands and options available on these tabs are restricted to only those that can be used to manipulate the objects the tab appears for. These tabs are displayed along with the core tabs of the ribbon and can be used to modify and format the objects that are displayed. You can switch between the contextual tabs and the core tabs as needed.

File Options and the View

.File- and print-related options are shown in Access 2010's *view*. The following is a summary of functions performed in the view

Command	Description of Function
Save	Save changes made within the current database.
Save Object As	Save the selected database object as a different database object, with a different name.
Save Database As	Save the current database with a new file name and/or location.
Open	Open a database.
Close Database	Close the current database.
Info	Access a number of options, including: • Share a database with other users. • Restrict access to other users • Define data relationships in tables. • Correct and fix database issues. • View object dependencies. • Analyze the performance of a database • View and edit database properties
Recent	View and open recently accessed databases.
New	Create a new blank database or one pre-populated with various elements based on a template.
Print	Preview and print an object, and select printer settings.
Save & Publish	Save the current database file to a variety of different output formats and options.
Help	View online and local help options and access the **Access Options** dialog box.
Options	Change Access configuration settings and preferences.

Command	Description of Function
Exit	Exit the Access application.

ACTIVITY 1-7
Exploring Access Ribbon Commands

Before You Begin
My Updated Database.accdb is open, and no database objects are opened in the document pane.

Scenario
To acquaint yourself with the location of Access' ribbon commands, and to get an overview of the variety of tasks you can perform in a database, you will take a quick tour of commands provided in the ribbon.

1. Explore commands available in the ribbon.

   a) Open tblInventory.
   b) Select each ribbon tab as you examine the groups of commands.

Tab	Description
Home tab	You will use commands in this tab for general editing and formatting tasks, as well as sorting, filtering, and searching.
Create tab	Use commands in this tab to create new database objects, such as tables, queries, forms, and reports.
External Data tab	Use commands in this tab to move large amounts of data into and out of Access. A wide variety of other data formats are supported, including Excel spreadsheets, text files, XML, PDF, and others.
Database Tools tab	Use commands in this tab to perform certain types of database-wide tasks.
Fields and Table tabs (**Table Tools**)	The tabs in this group are available only when a table is open and selected. Commands in these tabs apply only to tables.

2. Close the database and exit Access.

Tools and Applications Developed in Access

You can think of Access as a software construction set. You might use Access to create tools for yourself or for an entire team of data workers. Access includes tools that enable you to construct a user interface for a software application. In fact, some software developers use Access as a prototyping tool since it provides quick results with relatively little or no software programming code needed. By simply dragging and dropping objects onto a form, you can create elements that are commonly used in Windows applications, such as buttons, drop-down lists, list boxes, text boxes, check boxes, calendar date-pickers, and so forth.

Note: Access the LearnTO **Find Good Uses for Access** presentation from the **LearnTO** tile on the LogicalCHOICE Course screen.

TOPIC B

Create a Simple Access Database

You have opened and edited an existing database and have used objects that were created by someone else, including tables, forms, queries, and reports. There are a number of different ways you can create a database, such as starting totally from scratch with a blank database. But you can also stand on the shoulders of others who have created elaborate templates that do a lot of the heavy lifting for you, providing a nice "starter kit" for a wide variety of different types of databases.

Database Templates

You can use the database templates provided by Access as the model for a new database. Templates may include pre-defined tables, queries, forms, reports, layouts, fonts, themes, and other characteristics, which can save you considerable time over creating a blank database and adding those elements yourself. Many templates are provided by Microsoft. Additionally, Microsoft hosts a user community through which users can share templates they have created. You can access this community using your Windows Live® ID. Submissions to this site are checked for viruses and validated before they are posted, where they can be downloaded by users.

Save Options

The **File** tab includes three options for saving a database. The **Save Database As** command enables you to save an Access database to a different file name and location. The **Save & Publish** command presents various options that enable you to save the database in a different file format than the default Access 2010 version. The **Save** command updates the current database file with any changes you have made.

Field Definition

When you create a new database/tab, Access automatically creates an ID field that provides autonumbering to give each record a unique ID.

Design View

You can easily insert a new field in the **Datasheet** or **Design** view. In **Datasheet** view, you can add a field by selecting the data type for the field in a new column, and then you can name the field. **Design** view displays a grid in which you can define the structure of a table. Fields are shown along with their data types and descriptions.

Field Data Types

When you define a new field, you must specify the type of data the field will hold. The following are field types supported in Access.

Type	Description
Text	Text, digits, symbols, and other keyboard characters. This data type has a limit of 255 characters.
Memo	Similar content to text, but this type supports rich-text formatting, and can hold up to 2 GB of data.
Number	Numeric values only.
Date/Time	Formatted date and time values.

Type	Description
Currency	Monetary values, such as dollars, which are not rounded during calculations.
AutoNumber	Unique, sequential numbers created automatically by Access. Typically used to enable a field to contain a unique identifier.
Yes/No	Boolean values. The field can contain values such as **True/False**, **Yes/No**, or **On/Off**.
OLE Object	Binary data such as documents, images, and spreadsheets.
Hyperlink	Holds email addresses, web site URLs, and network paths.
Attachment	Holds file data. This field supports more file types than an Object Linking and Embedding (OLE) object, and enables multiple files to be attached to a record.
Calculated	Produces a result through calculation.
Lookup Wizard	Provides a list of selectable values.

Primary Key

A *primary key* is a field that is configured to require a unique value in each record. No two records in the table may have the same field value in the primary key field, and each record must contain a value in the primary key field. Because the field contains unique values, it can be used as a unique identifier for a record. Fields that are designated as a primary key are shown in **Design** view with a **Key** icon.

Object Naming Conventions

A naming convention is a set of rules for identifying and denoting certain variables and functions in Microsoft Access. Implementing a naming convention will likely increase readability and the aesthetic quality of your database. There are several naming conventions that different database administrators use, and not all agree on what is the best. The important thing is that you use one.

For example, one commonly-used naming convention is the Leszynski naming convention. This convention recommends that you not include spaces in field and table names. Although Access permits spaces, it will complicate matters for you later on if you start writing code or if you intend to use Access with other database systems. Names can be up to 64 characters long. If you do include spaces in object names, you can refer to the object in code by surrounding it in brackets to show that it is all part of the same object name. For example, a field name such as myFieldName does not require brackets, but a field name with spaces, such as [My Field Name], does.

 Access the Checklist tile on your LogicalCHOICE course screen for reference information and job aids on How to Create a New Database

ACTIVITY 1-8
Creating a New Database

Scenario

It's time to roll up your sleeves and create your own database. You will create an inventory tracking and ordering system for the Woodworker's Wheelhouse Store. To gain a good understanding of database construction, you will start from scratch rather than using a template, creating a blank database and building out its structure, functionality, and formatting.

1. Create a new database.
   a) Start the Microsoft Access application.
   b) Observe the Microsoft Access application window. Without a database open, Access begins in the **File** tab view, from which you can open an existing database or create a new one.

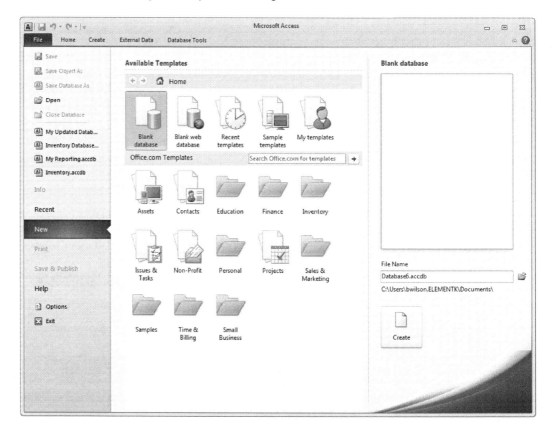

   c) In the **Available Templates** pane, select **Blank database**.
   d) In the **File Name** text box on the right side of the screen, change the file name to *My Inventory*.
   e) Select the **Browse** folder icon. Navigate to the C:\091001Data\Getting Started with Access folder and select **OK**.

File Name

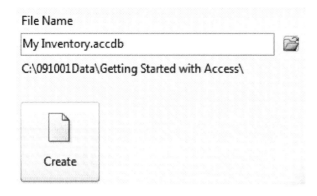

My Inventory.accdb

C:\091001Data\Getting Started with Access\

Create

f) Select **Create**. The database is created with one empty table, Table1.

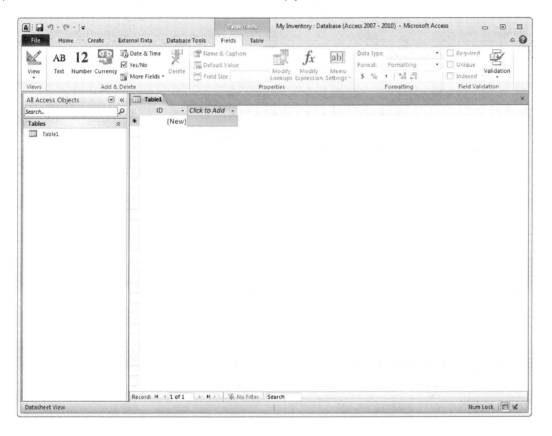

2. Define table fields.

a) Observe Table1. The first field, **ID**, has been automatically created. However, **ID** is an ambiguous field name so you will rename it.

b) Right-click the **ID** field header and select **Rename Field**.

c) Type *ProductCode*

d) Select the **Click to Add** column header and select **Text** to create a new field of type **Text**.

e) Rename **Field1** as *Dept*

f) Add another text field, naming it *SupplierID*

g) Add another text field, naming it *ItemDescription*

h) Select the **ItemDescription** column heading to choose the column.

i) Point between the **ItemDescription** and **Click to Add** column headings. The mouse pointer becomes a two-headed arrow to show that you can resize the column. Drag the **ItemDescription** column width wider, as shown.

 Caution: It can be tricky finding the right place to drag the column width. It's a little easier if you select the column first.

j) Select **File→Save** to save the database. Because the table has not been saved yet, you are prompted to name it before the database will be saved.

k) Select the table name, type *tblInventory*, and select **OK**.
l) Right-click the **tblInventory** tab and select **Design View**. The fields you created appear in a table. You can add fields within this view as well.
m) Select the table cell below **ItemDescription**.

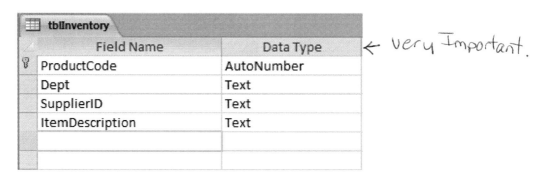

n) Type *UnitsInStock* and press **Enter**. The **Data Type** drop-down is selected. The **Text** data type is selected by default.
o) Select the drop-down arrow and select **Number**.
p) Add the following fields to the table.

Field Name	Data Type
TargetInventory	Number
ReorderLevel	Number
LastOrdered	Date/Time
Location	Text
Rack	Text
Origin	Text
OurUnitCost	Currency
RetailPrice	Currency

q) Observe the **Data Type** for **ProductCode**. The first field was automatically set to **AutoNumber**.

r) Change the **Data Type** for **ProductCode** to **Text**.
s) Observe the **Key** icon next to **ProductCode**. The icon shows that this field is a primary key, meaning that no two values entered within this field can be the same. The product code is a unique identifier in this table.
t) Save the database.
u) Right-click the **tblInventory** tab and select **Datasheet View**. The fields you created appear in the table.
v) Right-click the **tblInventory** tab and select **Close** to close the table while leaving the database open.

Methods to Create a Form

Access provides several methods for creating a form.

Form Creation Method	Description
Form	Create a form that automatically includes all the fields in the selected table or query.
Form Design	Start with a blank form in **Design** view and add components manually.
Blank Form	Start with a blank form in **Layout** view and add components manually.
Form Wizard	Create a form by selecting the tables or queries to use as the data source, and selecting each field to be included in the form.

Form Object Views

The following are descriptions of the various views Access provides for creating and using forms.

View	Use This View To
Form	Use a form to add, edit, and move among records.
Design	Create or modify elements of a form. In this view, you can add and delete form elements and set form properties.
Layout	Create or modify a form layout. This view presents data similar to the **Form** view, but enables you to change the form design, similar to the **Design** view. This view is optimized for making changes to the form's layout, such as resizing and rearranging form elements.

Form Sections

The form **Design** view divides the form into three sections: the **Header, Detail**, and **Footer**. These sections are customizable. The **Header** includes information you want to appear at the top of the form. Typically, this includes the form title. The **Detail** section includes the record data itself. The **Footer** section includes information you want to appear at the bottom of the form. Typically, this includes the date and page number.

 Access the Checklist tile on your LogicalCHOICE course screen for reference information and job aids on How to Create a Form

ACTIVITY 1-9
Creating and Testing a Form

Before You Begin

My Inventory.accdb is open, and no database objects are opened in the document pane.

Scenario

Much data will have to be entered in your database. To facilitate data entry, you will create a form for the tblInventory table.

---

1. Create a form.
   a) In the navigation pane, select **tblInventory** once to select it without opening it.
   b) Select **Create→Forms→Form**. A new form is created based on the table that was selected.
   c) Save the database. You are prompted to name the new form. The table's name is provided, but you will change it to have the frm (for "form") prefix.
   d) Name the form *frmInventory* and select **OK**.

2. Test the new form by entering a record.
   a) Right-click the **frmInventory** tab and select **Form View** to prepare the form for data entry.

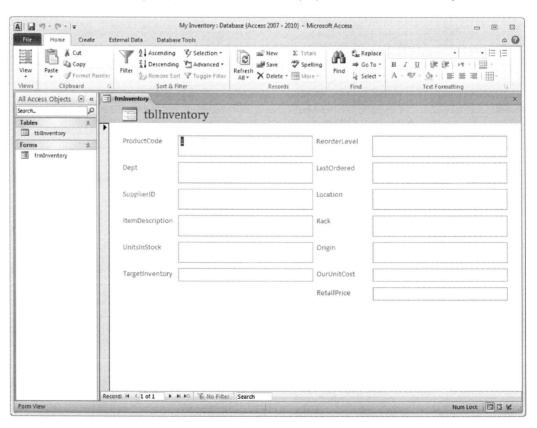

   b) Enter the following values into the form.

Field	Value
ProductCode	*bathhw-2*
Dept	*Bathroom*
SupplierID	*WOODSTOCK*
ItemDescription	*Windsor Model 24" Double Towel Bar Brushed Nickel*
UnitsInStock	*22*
TargetInventory	*25*
ReorderLevel	*10*
LastOrdered	*6/4/2012*
Location	*Showroom*
Rack	*2-3a*
Origin	*China*
OurUnitCost	*35*
RetailPrice	*41*

c) Observe what happened when you entered the **RetailPrice** value. A new record was automatically created. This behavior eliminates the step of having to request a new record, so you can quickly enter large numbers of records.

 Note: When you enter the date in the LastOrdered field, it will be displayed in the date/time format currently configured on your computer. Currency will be shown in the currency format.

d) Save the database.
e) Open the tblInventory table. Your data is displayed in the table layout.
f) Close the **tblInventory** and **frmInventory** tabs, and then close the My Inventory database.

TOPIC C

Get Help in Microsoft Access

As you work with Access, you may have questions about a particular feature or how to perform a specific task. The Access Help feature provides you with instructive information on Access. Its information sources include local files that are installed with Access, as well as resources located on the web.

Access Help

Access Help provides instructive information about Microsoft Access 2010 features and functionality. Some Help information is installed with Access on the local hard drive. Other Help information is located on the web. When you search, you can specify which sources you want to use.

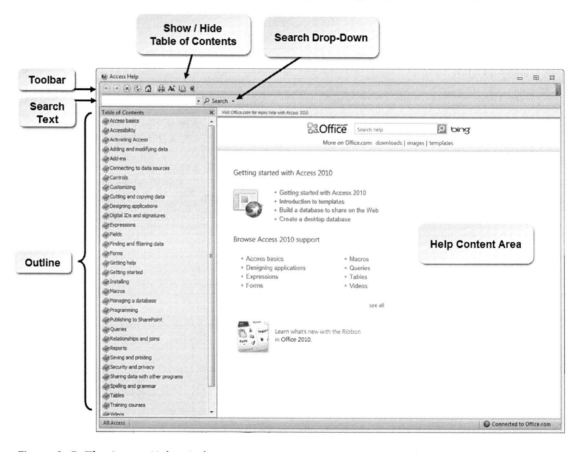

Figure 1–5: The Access Help window.

Access Help include various features to help you find answers to questions you have about using Access.

Help Feature	Description
Toolbar	Provides options to navigate, print, and format help content.
The **Search** text box	Enables you to type the text you want to search for.
The **Search** drop-down	Provides options to search online or offline content.

Help Feature	Description
Table of Contents	Displays topics available in Access Help. Navigate to a topic by clicking it.
The **Show/Hide Table of Contents** button	Toggles display of the Table of Contents. You can hide the Table of Contents to enlarge the area available for Help content.

You can press **F1** to access context-sensitive Help from within Access. Alternatively, you can use the **Search Access Help** drop-down list to narrow the search results to a specific area. Search categories include the following.

Area	What is Searched
Access Help	Built-in Help and Help on the Microsoft Office website.
Access Templates	Sample templates on the Microsoft Office website.
Access Training	Training resources on the Microsoft Office website.
All Access	All resources in Access Help, Access Templates, and Access Training.
Developer Reference	Programmers' guides, samples, and other resources related to programming in Access.

ACTIVITY 1–10
Getting Help in Access

Before You Begin
Access is running.

Scenario
Access is a widely used and well-supported application. Many support resources are available on the web and through developer communities. As you look for continued support, don't overlook the resources available to you through Access' integrated Help feature.

1. Navigate Help through the Table of Contents.
   a) Near the top-right corner of the Access application window, select the **Microsoft Access Help** button.

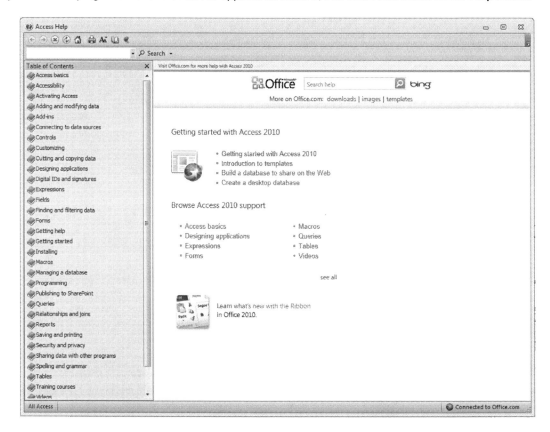

 Note: You can also press **F1** to launch the Access Help window. If the selected item in Access provides contextual help, the Help window will display help regarding that item.

   b) Select the **Maximize** button to maximize the Access Help window.

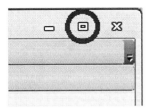

c) If the Table of Contents is not showing, then on the Access Help toolbar, select the **Show Table of Contents** button.

d) Observe the Access Help window. From this point, there are several ways to find the help topic you are looking for. You can browse the Table of Contents outline, use the Bing search bar, follow the topic links, or use the Access Help search bar.

e) In the **Table of Contents** pane, observe the various help topics that are displayed.

f) Select the **Access basics** link.

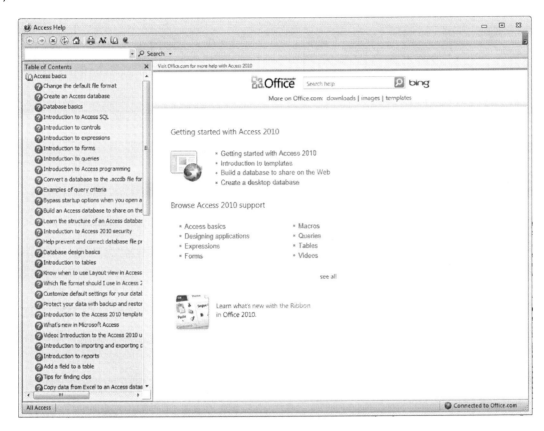

The outline expands to show topics under that heading.

g) In the Access basics section, select the **Create an Access database** link.

h) Briefly observe the article that appears in the right pane. Scroll as needed.

2. Search for a Help topic.

a) In the **Search** text box in the upper-left corner of the Access Help window, type *browse records*

b) Select the **Search** drop-down arrow. Sources that can be searched are listed.

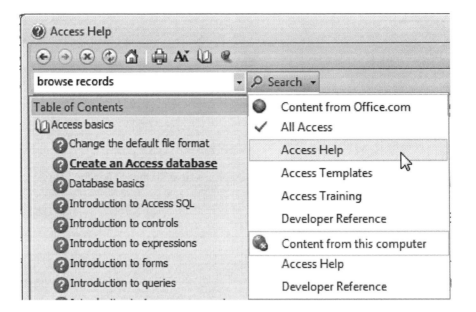

c) Select **Access Help** and select **Search**.
d) Select **Find records in an Access database**. An article explaining how to navigate records in Access is shown.

3. Use the Help system to find a general summary of a database design process. Discuss the following question.

    What are the first three steps of a database design process?

4. Close the **Access Help** window.

Summary

In this lesson, you systematically analyzed and used an existing Access database to learn how an Access database is constructed. You used existing tables, queries, forms, and reports. You considered potential uses for Access and developed a simple database from scratch, including a form. And, you used the Help system to look up help on navigation within Access and guidelines on database design.

Describe the general tasks involved in constructing a database.

What are some of the benefits of moving data into a database application like Access?

 Note: Check your LogicalCHOICE Course screen for opportunities to interact with your classmates, peers, and the larger LogicalCHOICE online community about the topics covered in this course or other topics you are interested in. From the Course screen you can also access available resources for a more continuous learning experience.

2 Working with Table Data

Lesson Time: 1 hour, 10 minutes

Lesson Objectives

In this lesson, you will work with table data. You will:

- Efficiently locate and change data.

- Sort and filter records in a table.

- Create a lookup field.

Lesson Introduction

You are familiar with the Microsoft® Office Access® 2010 user interface and have created a simple database. Simply by moving your data into Access data tables, you gain access to powerful capabilities for working with structured data, such as searching, sorting, filtering, and providing cross-table lookups. In this lesson, you will use those capabilities as you manage the content within a product database.

TOPIC A

Modify Table Data

You created the basic table structure within a database. To keep data in these tables current, you need to know how to add, delete, and update data in a table.

Autocorrect

Like other Microsoft® Office applications, Access provides an Autocorrect feature. Access provides corrections to common formatting or spelling problems. On occasion, you may wish to override this feature, and can do so by selecting the **Lightning Bolt** icon that Access shows next to a word it has changed through Autocorrect. A menu is shown with an option to change the item back to your original spelling.

Commit, Save, and Undo

When you enter data in a record, the new data is not committed to storage until you leave the record —by moving to another record, for example. Access displays a **Pencil** icon when you have uncommitted data. To commit data without moving to another record, you can save the database or click the **Pencil** icon. You can "back out" of the new data by pressing **Esc** or selecting **Undo**.

 Access the Checklist tile on your LogicalCHOICE course screen for reference information and job aids on How to Undo

ACTIVITY 2-1
Undoing Record Modifications

Data Files

C:\091001Data\Working with Table Data\Inventory Modify.accdb

 Note: Depending on your computer's system configuration, you may not see the .accdb file-name extension.

Scenario

As you type, Access monitors your spelling and automatically makes changes. Often, those changes are helpful, but sometimes you want to keep the text the way your originally entered it. Fortunately, it's easy to back out of an Autocorrect change. If you make changes that you need to undo, the **Undo** command works in Access much as it does in other Office applications.

---

1. Open the Inventory Modify database and display the tblInventory table. If a security prompt is shown, select **Enable Content**.

2. Save the database in C:\091001\Working with Table Data as *My Inventory Modify*. If necessary, close the open objects. Select **Enable Content**, if prompted.

3. Add a new record to the tblInventory table.
   a) Re-open the tblInventory table.
   b) Select **Home→Records→New**.
   c) Observe that the input focus has moved to first column of the new record row (the last record plus one row).

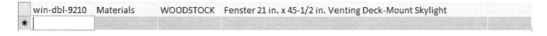

   d) Type *dec-25* and press **Enter**.
      The next field, Dept, is selected.
   e) Type *Decor* and press **Enter**.
   f) Observe that Access automatically corrects the spelling, adding an acute mark over the letter E.

   g) Select the **Autocorrect (Lightning Bolt)** icon and select **Change Back to "Decor"**.

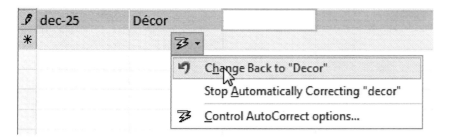

h) Press **Enter** to enter "Decor" and advance to the next field.

4. Exit the record without committing.

a) Observe the **Pencil** icon at the left end of the record. The record has not yet been written.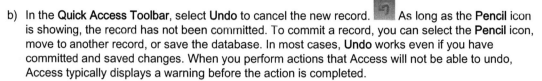

b) In the **Quick Access Toolbar**, select **Undo** to cancel the new record. As long as the **Pencil** icon is showing, the record has not been committed. To commit a record, you can select the **Pencil** icon, move to another record, or save the database. In most cases, **Undo** works even if you have committed and saved changes. When you perform actions that Access will not be able to undo, Access typically displays a warning before the action is completed.

Quick Search

In addition to providing buttons to navigate from record to record, the Record navigation bar provides a **Search** text box that moves you to the first record that contains the text you type, as soon as you enter it.

 Access the Checklist tile on your LogicalCHOICE course screen for reference information and job aids on **How to Use Quick Search to Find and Modify Records**

Search box @ bottom of screen
- searches data

Search box on upper left
- searches left column menu
      table, Querys etc.

ACTIVITY 2-2
Using Quick Search to Find and Modify Records

Before You Begin

The My Inventory Modify database is open and tblInventory is displayed in **Datasheet** view.

Scenario

Your product line and inventory are continually changing. On a regular basis, you and your employees must update your database to keep information current. Access provides a quick search feature to help you quickly jump to the record you need to change.

1. Update a record in the tblInventory table.

   a) In the **Record** navigation bar **Search** text box, type *hinge-16*

As you type, the first record that matches information you have typed is selected, and as you add more letters, the selected information changes. Searching on a value that is likely to be unique (such as a product ID) ensures you will find the record quickly.

   b) In the **SupplierID** field for the selected record, type *WOODSTOCK* and press **Enter**.

   c) Press **Home** to move the input focus back to the first field (**ProductCode**) of the current record.

2. Delete a record from the Inventory table.

   a) In the **Record** navigation bar **Search** text box, type *hinge-47* to find the record for hinge-47.

   b) Move the mouse pointer to the left of hinge-47, and when it changes to an arrow, right-click and select **Delete Record**.

   c) In the **Microsoft Access** message box, select **Yes**. The record is deleted.

The Find and Replace Dialog Box

The **Find and Replace** dialog box enables you to quickly locate and change database information. The dialog box contains two tabs with options that enable you to search for and replace data.

Tab	Description
Find	Identify text to be found in the **Find What** text box. You can also specify the search target, as well as the search direction.
Replace	Identify text to be replaced in the **Replace With** text box. Provide the replacement text, the search target, as well as the search direction.

 Access the Checklist tile on your LogicalCHOICE course screen for reference information and job aids on How to Use Find and Replace

ACTIVITY 2-3
Using Find and Replace to Modify Records

Before You Begin
The My Inventory Modify database is open, and tblInventory is displayed in **Datasheet** view.

Scenario
Sometimes you need to make the same change to multiple records. If the change is consistent and pervasive, you might be able to use **Find and Replace** to make the change.

---

1. Replace all instances of the text "dec-" with "hmdecor-".
    a) Scroll to view records in the Décor department.
    b) Observe that **ProductCodes** for the Décor department begin with "dec-", while **ProductCodes** for the Deck Patio department begin with "deck-". These two product code prefixes are similar and may lead to data entry errors. To avoid confusion, you will change the prefix for Home Decor items to "hmdecor-".
    c) Select the **ProductCode** table heading to select the whole column. You will limit your search to this column.
    d) Select **Home→Find→Replace**.

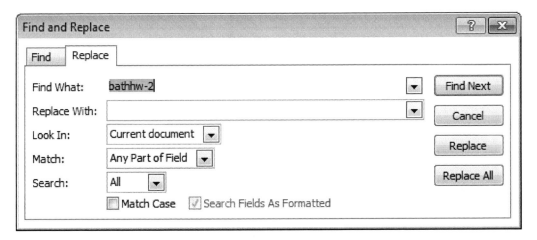

    e) Verify that, within the **Find and Replace** dialog box, the **Replace** tab is selected.

 Note: The same dialog box is used for both find and replace operations, so it is good practice to verify that the tab you have selected matches the operation you want to perform

    f) In the **Find What** text box, type *dec-* and press **Tab**.
    g) In the **Replace With** text box, type *hmdecor-*
    h) From the **Look In** drop-down list, select **Current field**.
    i) From the **Match** drop-down list, select **Start of Field**.

j) Select **Replace All** to replace all the instances of the text "dec-" with the text "hmdecor-".

k) In the **Microsoft Access** message box, select **Yes**.

l) In the **Find and Replace** dialog box, select the **Close** button.

2. Scroll the table, if necessary, to verify that all instances of the dec- **ProductCodes** have been changed to hmdecor-.

Datasheet Totals

Use the **Totals** row to add summary values to a table. The **Totals** row enables you to display a calculated value based on all the values in a specified field, such as the count of records or the sum, average, maximum, minimum, standard deviation, or variance of values in the field.

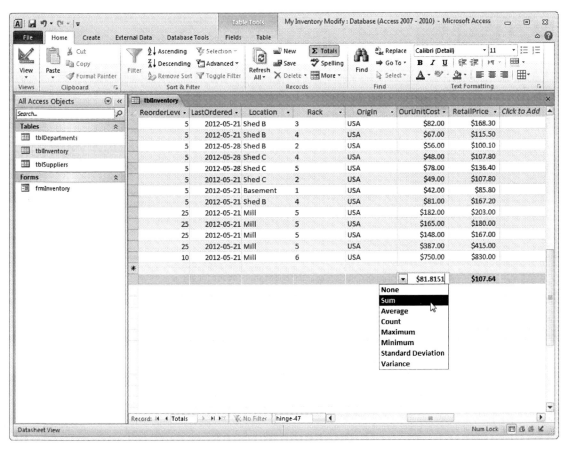

Figure 2-1: Adding calculations to the Totals row.

Access the Checklist tile on your LogicalCHOICE course screen for reference information and job aids on **How to Add a Totals Row**

ACTIVITY 2-4
Adding a Totals Row to a Datasheet

Before You Begin
The My Inventory Modify database is open, and tblInventory is displayed in **Datasheet** view.

Scenario
As you modify records in a table, it can be helpful to have summary information provided right in the table so you can see the general effect of your changes on record count, averages, and so forth, without having to run a report. The **Totals** row can provide such information.

---

1. Add a **Total** row to the tblInventory table.
   a) Scroll to the bottom of tblInventory, and observe that there is currently no **Totals** row.
   b) Select **Home→Records→Totals**.
   c) Observe that a new row labeled "Total" is shown at the bottom of the table.

2. Configure the **Total** row.
   a) In the **Total** row, select the **Dept** column, and from the drop-down list, select **Count**.
   b) Observe that the number of products is shown, not the number of departments.
   c) In the **Total** row, select the **OurUnitCost** column, and from the drop-down list, select **Average**.

    Note: When you scroll to the right, the **Total** row heading may scroll out of view. If you cannot produce the drop-down list, you may be selecting in the wrong row. The **Total** row is right beneath the * row.

   d) Observe that the average cost of products is shown.
   e) In the **Total** row, show the average **RetailPrice**.

3. Save the table.

TOPIC B

Sort and Filter Records

As you work with a database, it can be helpful to temporarily sort or filter a table to show only records that match certain criteria. For example, you might want to quickly view the products for a particular vendor. If this were a repetitive task, a query might be called for, but sometimes you just need to quickly focus on a particular group of records. Access provides some powerful features that enable you to quickly accomplish this.

The Sort Feature

Access's sorting capability can automatically arrange numeric, alphabetic, or date values in ascending or descending order. Once applied, you can remove a sort when it's no longer needed.

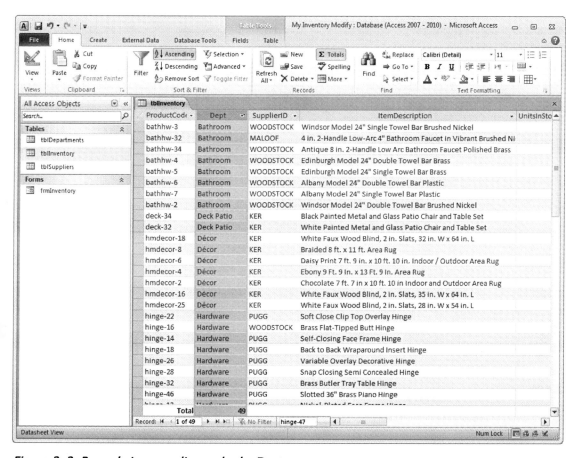

Figure 2-2: Records in ascending order by Dept.

The Filter Feature

Access enables you to filter data based on criteria you have applied to a specific column. This enables you to focus only on records that meet certain criteria, such as maintenance tasks that are overdue (based on the last maintenance date), or products that need to be ordered from a supplier (based on the current amount of inventory). You can specify a different filter for each field in the table, applying multiple filters at the same time.

Filter Commands

The following are commands provided in the **Sort & Filter** ribbon group.

Option	Description
The **Selection** drop-down list	Enables you to filter items within a selected field. The drop-down list provides various options to filter data based on the values in the field, values not in the field, or values within a specific range.
The **Advanced** drop-down list	From this option, you can apply filters not commonly available in the filters list or save a filter as a query object in a database.
The **Toggle Filter** button	Enables you to switch between a filtered and unfiltered view of data.

Saving a Filter as a Query

A filter remains applied only as long as the table remains open. When you reopen a table, you have to reapply the filter if you want it in effect. However, you can save a filtered table as a query, which you can open the next time you want to view the filtered table.

 Access the Checklist tile on your LogicalCHOICE course screen for reference information and job aids on How to Sort and Filter Records

ACTIVITY 2-5
Sorting and Filtering Records

Before You Begin
The My Inventory Modify database is open, and tblInventory is displayed in **Datasheet** view.

Scenario
You are considering switching from the vendor WOODSTOCK to a different vendor. You want to quickly determine how many products will be affected.

---

1. Sort tblInventory by **Dept** and **SupplierID**.
   a) Observe that tblInventory is not sorted by **Dept** or **SupplierID**.
   b) Select the **Dept** table heading to select the column.
   c) Select **Home→Sort & Filter→Ascending**.

   Records are now sorted by department. A **Sort Indicator** icon appears in the column heading for **Dept**, showing that a sort is in effect.

   d) Select the **SupplierID** table heading to select the column.
   e) Select **Home→Sort & Filter→Ascending**.
   f) Observe how the table is sorted. The **Sort Indicator** icon appears in the **Dept** and **SupplierID** headings, showing that a sort is in effect for both columns. Since the sort was applied to **SupplierID** last, that is the *primary sort*. **Dept** is a *secondary sort*. Within the group of records for the PUGG **SupplierID**, the records are sorted by **Dept**: a group of Hardware records is followed by Materials records. Note that additional Materials records appear in the records for the WOODSTOCK **SupplierID**.

2. Remove both sorts from tblInventory.
   a) Observe the various departments that are supplied by PUGG and WOODSTOCK. This database is small enough that you could manually count the number of products supplied by each vendor, but it would be faster (especially if this were a much larger database) to filter out records by **SupplierID** and let Access do the counting for you.
   b) Select **Home→Sort & Filter→Remove Sort** to restore the table to its original sort order.

3. Filter tblInventory by **Supplier**.
   a) Select the **SupplierID** table heading to select the column.
   b) Select **Home→Sort & Filter→Filter**.
   c) In the displayed drop-down list, uncheck the **(Select All)** check box.
   d) Check the **WOODSTOCK** check box and select **OK**.
   e) Observe that only the products supplied by WOODSTOCK are shown. A **Filter** icon appears in the **SupplierID** column heading to show that a filter has been applied based on that column. There are 13 products in total.

4. Add a filter for the Materials department.
   a) Observe the departments in the **Dept** column. Several departments are supplied by WOODSTOCK. You can run a second filter to further filter down the table.
   b) Select the **Down-Arrow** icon in the **Dept** column heading.

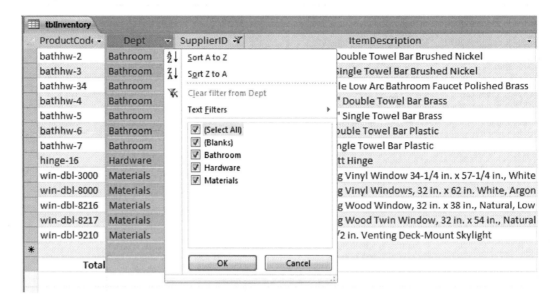

This is an alternative to selecting the column and selecting **Home→Filter**.

   c) In the displayed drop-down list, uncheck the **(Select All)** check box.

   d) Check the **Materials** check box and select **OK**.

   e) Observe that both the **Dept** and **SupplierID** column headings both contain a **Filter** icon, showing that both filters are in effect. There are five products supplied by WOODSTOCK for the Materials department.

5. Clear the **Dept** filter.

   a) Select the **Filter** icon in the **Dept** table heading.

   b) Select **Clear filter from Dept**.

   c) Observe that the **Dept** filter has been cleared. The **SupplierID** filter is still applied.

   d) Save the database and exit Access.

   e) Reopen the My Inventory Modify.accdb database.

   f) Double-click the **tblInventory** table to select it.

g) Observe that the filter is no longer applied. Filters applied through the **Sort & Filter** group commands are not saved along with the database. You can use them to temporarily narrow down and organize tables, knowing that the original data in the table will remain intact when you save.

h) Close tblInventory but leave the database open.

TOPIC C

Create Lookups

Early databases were flat files. They contained one set of data and were not necessarily very organized. While it is possible to create single-table databases in Access, things start to get interesting when you structure data in multiple tables and establish relationships between those tables. Lookup fields enable you to establish a simple relationship between two tables and provide a first step toward developing more advanced table relationships.

Lookup Fields

Many Access features require that field values be entered consistently. For example, Access will not view "WOODSTOCK," "Woodstock," and "WDSTK" as the same values. If you provide a fixed set of values to choose from rather than have the user enter them in a record through freeform text entry, you will promote consistency.

Table Relationships

Access provides many powerful features that enable you to quickly search, sort, and filter table data. You can do these tasks on a table-by-table basis, but Access also provides advanced capabilities that enable you to deal with multiple tables in unison. This opens up all sorts of possibilities for improving efficiency, maintainability, and performance of the database.

Once you establish a *relationship* between tables, you can work with the data in those tables in unison. For example, your suppliers table might contain a list of product suppliers and information such as the supplier ID, contact information, and so forth. Your inventory table might contain a list of products you carry, along with related information such as the product code and the supplier ID of the company from which you buy the product. Since both tables include a supplier ID field, you could use that field to establish a relationship between the two tables.

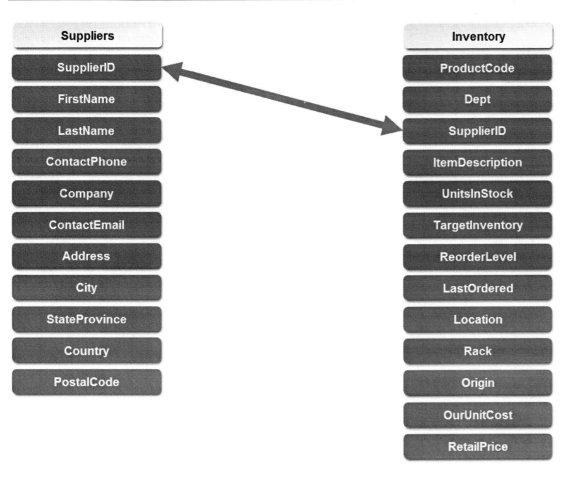

Figure 2-3: A table relationship.

Suppose you have a product code for one of the products in inventory. In the inventory table, you can look up that product's associated supplier ID. Once you know the supplier ID, you can look up the supplier's name, phone number, and address. So knowing the product code can lead you to information about the supplier for that product, even though the supplier information is in a different table.

There is elegance to this approach. You could provide contact information fields directly in the inventory table, and enter it for each product. But that requires a lot of duplication of data and effort, and would be difficult to maintain. With related tables, once the relationship is established through a common field, the data from one table is associated with records in the other table without the need for duplication.

The Relationships View

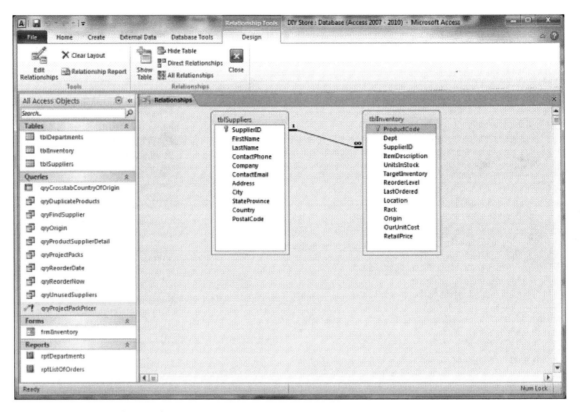

Figure 2-4: The Relationships view.

The **Relationships** view shows the relationships that exist between various tables in a database. A field list is shown for each table, and join lines connect related tables. Each end of the join line will display either the number 1 (read as "one") or an infinity symbol (read as "many"). This indicates the relationship (one-to-one or one-to-many) between the two tables. "One" means that the field in that table must contain unique data. Access will not permit duplicate values on that side of the relationship. "Many" means that the field in that table can contain duplicate values.

Foreign Key

A *foreign key* is a field that is linked to the primary key in another table. In the example shown in the figure, tblInventory contains the foreign key field **SupplierID**, which is linked to the primary key field **SupplierID** in tblSuppliers. To establish such a link, the primary key and foreign key fields must have the same data type. Duplicate values can appear in foreign key fields, but unique values must exist in primary key fields.

Referential Integrity

A database is considered to have *referential integrity* when every foreign key in every table has a link to a primary key in another table. Ensuring referential integrity prevents invalid data entry.

 Note: Access the LearnTO **Follow Principles of Database Design** presentation from the **LearnTO** tile on the LogicalCHOICE Course screen.

ACTIVITY 2-6
Examining the Purpose of a Primary Key

Before You Begin

The My Inventory Modify database is open. No objects are displayed in the document pane.

Scenario

In this activity, you will conduct an experiment to see what happens if you enter values that are not unique within a field defined as a primary key.

Examine how Access enforces the uniqueness of a primary key.

a) Display tblSuppliers in **Design** view.

   The **SupplierID** field provides a unique identifier for each supplier in the table. The **Key** icon shows that **SupplierID** is the primary key for tblSuppliers.

b) View tblSuppliers in **Datasheet** view.
c) Observe the supplier records. Each supplier has a specific **SupplierID**, as well as other information.
d) In **SupplierID**, select the value **WRIGHT**.
e) Change **WRIGHT** to *WOODSTOCK*

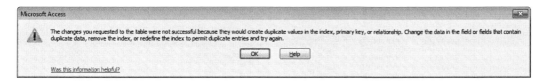

f) Press **Enter**.
g) Select **File→Save**.

![Microsoft Access dialog: The changes you requested to the table were not successful because they would create duplicate values in the index, primary key, or relationship. Change the data in the field or fields that contain duplicate data, remove the index, or redefine the index to permit duplicate entries and try again. OK Help. Was this information helpful?]

   You cannot save the change you made because the primary key for the table would contain duplicate values. A primary key is a field that contains unique values in every record. Many of Access' most powerful features rely on tables having a primary key field. Using these key fields, you can establish a "lookup relationship" between one table and another.

h) Select **OK** and select **Undo** to revert the record back to **WRIGHT**.
i) Close the **tblSuppliers** tab.

The Property Sheet Pane

Use the *Property Sheet* to set properties for objects such as tables, queries, forms, and reports. The **Property Sheet** is available only in **Design** view.

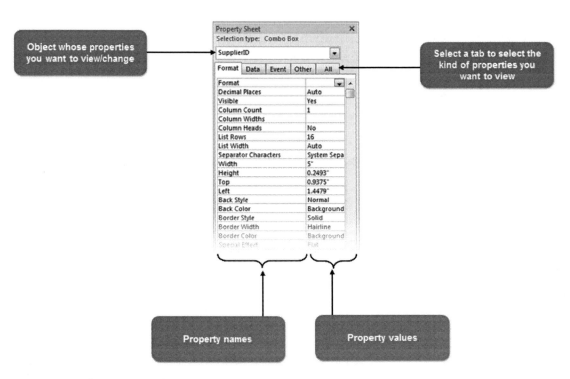

Figure 2-5: The Property Sheet.

ACTIVITY 2-7
Configuring a Form Lookup Field

Before You Begin
The My Inventory Modify database is open. No objects are displayed in the document pane.

Scenario
You want to add some features in your entry form to prevent users from entering duplicate values in a primary key field.

1. In frmInventory, enter a supplier code that doesn't exist in tblSuppliers.
   a) In the navigation pane, double-click **frmInventory** to show the entry form.
   b) Observe the **SupplierID** code for the bathhw-2 record. At this point, the **SupplierID** is a freeform text entry field. Users can freely type values other than those in tblSuppliers.
   c) Change the **SupplierID** for bathhw-2 to *BLUEBIRD*
   d) Save the database. Access has not prevented you from entering a name that is not in tblSuppliers. At this point, there is no relationship between the supplier IDs in tblSuppliers and the supplier IDs in tblInventory.
   e) Select **Undo** to change the **SupplierID** for bathhw-2 from **BLUEBIRD** back to **WOODSTOCK**.
   f) Save the database. Before you enforce perfect matching between the supplier IDs in both tables, you must ensure that any values already entered are a match.

2. Establish a lookup relationship between frmInventory and tblSuppliers.
   a) Right-click the **frmInventory** tab and select **Design View**.
   b) Right-click the **SupplierID** text box and select **Change To→Combo Box**.
   c) Observe the **SupplierID** combo box. Depending on the area your monitor displays, you may need to scroll right to observe that a drop-down arrow has been added.
   d) If the **Property Sheet** is not showing, then select **Design→Tools→Property Sheet** to display it.

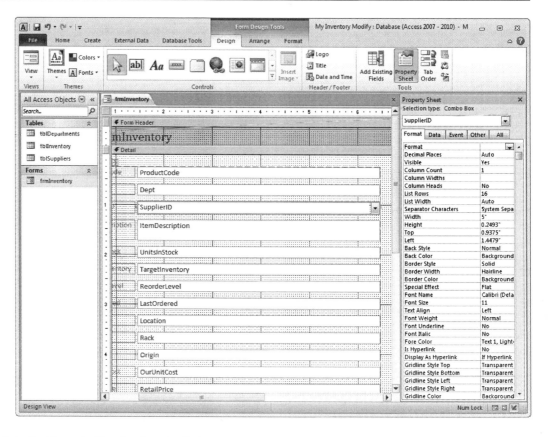

e) In the **Property Sheet**, select the **Data** tab to show only properties related to data.

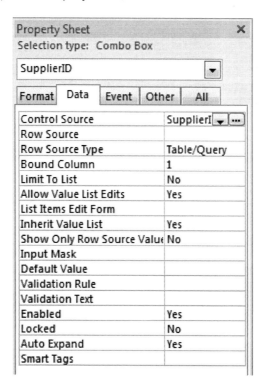

f) In the **Property Sheet**, select **Row Source** to display a drop-down box, and select **tblSuppliers**. The **SupplierID** drop-down list will now be populated by the first column in tblSuppliers.

g) Save the database.

3. Test the lookup field.

a) Display frmInventory in **Form View**.

b) Select the drop-down arrow for **SupplierID**. The supplier list is shown.

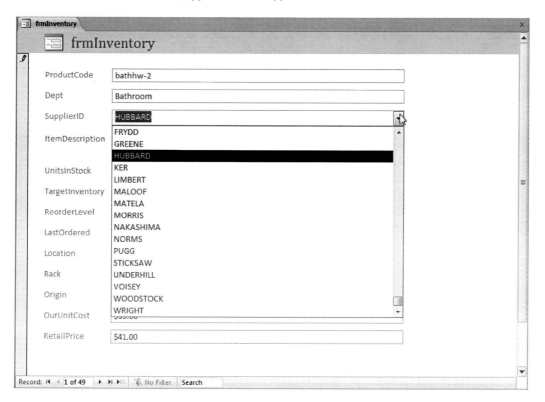

c) Select **HUBBARD**. The value **HUBBARD** now appears in the **SupplierID** field. This feature will help users select just the acceptable field values.

d) Save the database.

4. Test text entry into the **SupplierID** combo box.

a) Type the following value into the **SupplierID** combo box: *BLUEBIRD*

b) Save the database. Unfortunately, a combo box also permits text entry.

Note: The name "combo box" is used because it is a combination between a list and a text box. You need to anticipate that users may enter values by picking *or* by typing.

c) Revert the value of **SupplierID** to **WOODSTOCK**.

d) Close frmInventory.

5. Establish a relationship between tblInventory and tblSuppliers.

a) Select **Database Tools→Relationships**.

b) Select **tblInventory** and select **Add**.

c) Select **tblSuppliers** and select **Add**.

d) Select **Close**. The **tblInventory** and **tblSuppliers** field lists are shown.

e) Drag the bottom edge of each field list to size so you can see all fields in both lists.

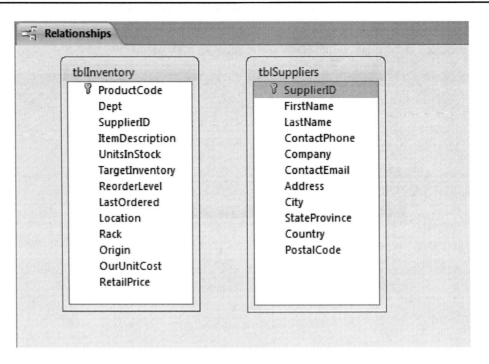

f) Drag **SupplierID** from tblInventory onto **SupplierID** in tblSuppliers. The **Edit Relationships** dialog box is shown.

g) Check **Enforce Referential Integrity**.

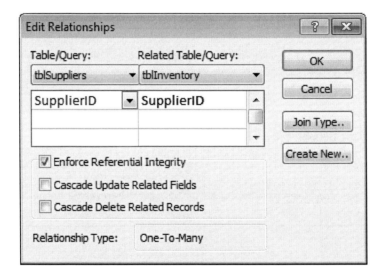

h) Select **Create**.

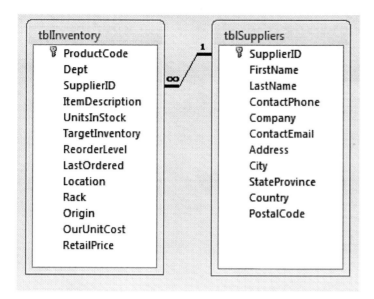

You established a relationship through the **SupplierID** fields in tblInventory and tblSuppliers. Access now has a way to enforce the referential integrity between these two tables. In other words, Access won't permit the user to enter a value in tblInventory's **SupplierID** field that doesn't exist in tblSuppliers.

i) Select **Design→Close**.

j) Select **Yes** to save the relationship layout changes you made.

6. Attempt to enter an invalid **SupplierID** with referential integrity enforced.

a) Display **frmInventory**.

b) Select the value in the **SupplierID** combo box and type *BLUEBIRD* to replace it.

c) Save the database.

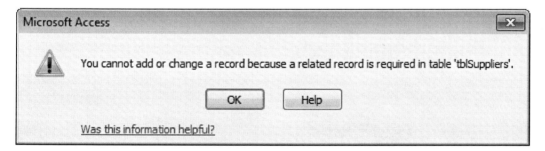

Access now prevents you from entering a name that is not in tblSuppliers. A relationship now exists between the **SupplierID** in tblSuppliers and **SupplierID** in tblInventory. Access enforces the referential integrity of that relationship.

d) Select **OK** and press **Esc** to revert the record back to **WOODSTOCK**.

e) Close frmInventory and the My Inventory Modify database.

7. Consider the following questions and jot down your responses. Try to use your own words rather than re-capping what is written in your student guide.

What is the benefit of establishing a lookup field?

8. **What is the benefit of establishing a table relationship and enforcing referential integrity?**

Summary

In this lesson, you learned how to add, delete, and update data in a table, including making mass content updates through Access' **Find and Replace** feature. You learned how to temporarily sort or filter a table to show only records that match certain criteria, and you created lookup fields, which is a first step toward developing more advanced table relationships.

When might you use the Find dialog box instead of a query?

Why might a lookup field be beneficial?

 Note: Check your LogicalCHOICE Course screen for opportunities to interact with your classmates, peers, and the larger LogicalCHOICE online community about the topics covered in this course or other topics you are interested in. From the Course screen you can also access available resources for a more continuous learning experience.

3 | Querying a Database

Lesson Time: 1 hour

Lesson Objectives

In this lesson, you will query a database. You will:

- Join data from different tables through a query.

- Sort and filter data through a query.

- Perform calculations through a query.

Lesson Introduction

You have created a database, populated tables, and have made updates to database content. You have searched, sorted, and filtered datasheets and have configured fields to look up data in other tables. As powerful as those features are, however, they are limited. They are temporary and easily overwritten. In this lesson, you will see how queries enable you to create reusable instructions that perform complex operations on dynamic table data lightning fast and precisely the same way each time. Queries also provide the added benefit of enabling you to join data from multiple tables on the fly.

TOPIC A

Join Data from Different Tables in a Query

As you continue to work with Microsoft® Office Access® databases, you will appreciate how important it is organize data within multiple related tables. Sometimes, however, you need to display data from multiple tables in a single view. Joining data from multiple tables is one of the significant tasks that can be accomplished using a query.

Query Object Views

The following are descriptions of the various views Access provides for creating and using query objects.

View	Use This View To
Datasheet	Display the query result in a table.
PivotTable	Create PivotTables from the query result.
PivotChart	Create PivotCharts from the query result.
SQL	Write SQL query statements directly or view the SQL statements that Access has constructed based on query options you have selected.
Design	Construct a query using visual tools.

The Simple Query Wizard

The *Simple Query Wizard* prompts you through steps to create a query. Despite its name, you can use this wizard to create fairly complex queries, joining data from multiple tables and other queries. As you select each source table or query, the wizard presents a list of available fields, which you can select to include in the new query.

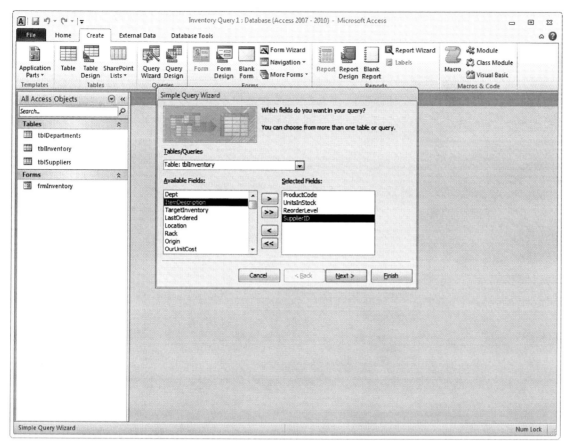

Figure 3-1: The Simple Query Wizard.

Types of Queries

The **Query Wizard** dialog box enables you to create various types of queries.

Query Type	Description
Simple	Creates a new query by enabling you to select fields from one or more tables and queries.
Crosstab	Creates a new crosstab query, which displays data grouped by category in a way that may help in summarizing results or identifying patterns in data.
Find duplicates	Creates a new query that shows records from a table or query that have duplicate field values.
Find unmatched	Creates a new query that shows records in one table or query that have no related records in another table or query. This can be useful in finding unused records that can be deleted or archived.

The Run Command

Use the *Run command* to launch a query from the query **Design** view. Select
Design→Results→Run to launch a query.

Note: Alternatively, you can run a query by double-clicking the query name in the navigation pane.

 Access the Checklist tile on your **LogicalCHOICE** course screen for reference information and job aids on **How to Create a Query by Using the Query Wizard**

ACTIVITY 3-1
Creating a Query by Using the Query Wizard

Data Files

C:\091001Data\Querying a Database\Inventory Query 1.accdb

Scenario

You want to produce a view of your data that combines elements from the inventory and supplier tables. You can do that with a query since the two tables already have an established relationship through the **SupplierID** field.

---

1. Open the Inventory Query 1 database. If a security prompt is shown, select **Enable Content**.

2. Save the database in C:\091001Data\Querying a Database as *My Inventory Query 1* and select **Enable Content** if you are prompted.

3. Launch the **Simple Query Wizard**.
   a) Select **Create→Queries→Query Wizard**.

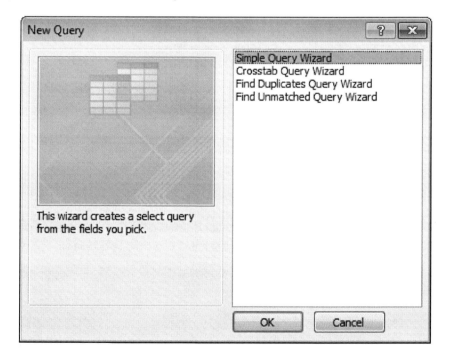

   b) In the **New Query** dialog box, verify that **Simple Query Wizard** is selected and select **OK**. You are prompted to specify which fields will be included in the result of the query. Results can come from more than one table.

4. Select the fields that will be displayed in the query results.
   a) From the **Tables/Queries** drop-down list, select **Table: tblInventory**.
   b) In the **Available Fields** list box, double-click **ProductCode** to move it to the **Selected Fields** list box.
   c) Move the following additional fields to the **Selected Fields** list box.

   • **UnitsInStock**

- ReorderLevel
- SupplierID

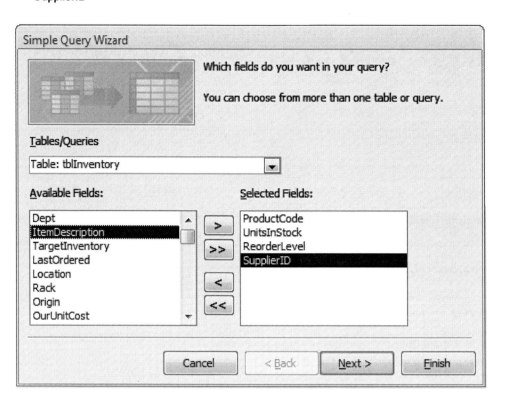

d) From the **Tables/Queries** drop-down list, select **Table: tblSuppliers**.
e) Move the following additional fields to the **Selected Fields** list box.
- FirstName
- LastName
- ContactPhone
- ContactEmail
f) Select **Next**. You are prompted to choose between a detail or summary query.

5. Finish the query and view the results.
a) Observe that the **Detail (shows every field of every record)** option is selected and select **Next**. You are prompted to enter a title for the query.
b) Change the text in the **What title do you want for your query?** text box to *qryProductSupplierDetail*
c) Observe that the **Open the query to view information** option is chosen and select **Finish**. The query results are shown.

d) Close qryProductSupplierDetail.

6. Save the database.

Query Design

Use the *Query Design* feature to create a new query in **Design** view. Add tables and queries to the **Design** view to display field lists. Then add fields from the field lists to the query design grid. This view also enables you to specify criteria, sorts, and summary data that will be included in the query.

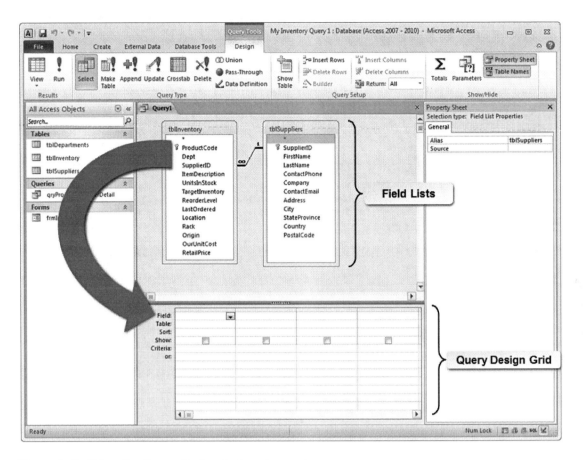

Figure 3-2: Using the Query Design feature to create a query.

When you are in the query's **Design** view, command groups under the **Design** contextual tab provide tools to enable you to create and modify queries.

Group	Provides Tools To
Results	Change the query view and execute a query.
Query type	Identify query types used to select, append, update, or delete records. Create crosstab queries and use other advanced options.
Query setup	Insert and delete rows and columns, use the *Expression Builder* to build expressions and use various advanced query setup options.
Show/hide	Show or hide various query elements.

 Access the Checklist tile on your LogicalCHOICE course screen for reference information and job aids on How to Create a Query by Using Query Design

ACTIVITY 3-2
Creating a Query by Using Query Design

Before You Begin
The My Inventory Query 1 database is open. No objects are open in the document pane.

Scenario
You will create a query that give you information you need to compile your weekly product orders. You will start by building a query that joins two tables. Rather than use a query wizard, you will go directly into **Design** view and create the query there.

---

1. Create a query.
   a) Select **Create→Queries→Query Design**. The **Show Table** dialog box prompts you to select the tables whose fields will be involved in this query.
   b) In the **Show Table** dialog box, on the **Tables** tab, select **tblInventory**. Then hold down **Ctrl** and select **tblSuppliers**. Both tables should be selected.

   c) Select **Add**.
   d) Select **Close** to close the dialog box.
   e) Resize and move the field lists, if necessary, to see all of the fields. Close the **Property Sheet** if you need more room.
   f) Observe the table relationships shown in the Query1 **Design** view. The tblSuppliers and tblInventory tables are related through **SupplierID**. The tblDepartments table is not related to the other tables.
   g) In the tblInventory field list, double-click **ProductCode** to add it to the query design grid.

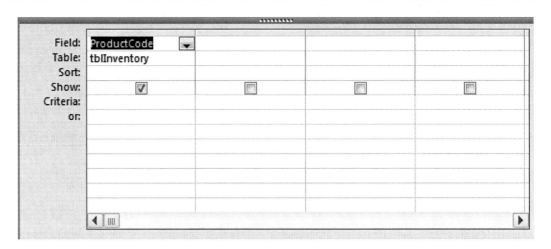

h) Similarly, add the following fields to the query design grid.
- ItemDescription
- UnitsInStock
- ReorderLevel
- TargetInventory
- OurUnitCost
- SupplierID

i) Add the following fields from tblSuppliers to the query design grid.
- Company
- FirstName
- LastName

j) Save the database. You are prompted to provide a query name.

k) Type *qryReorderNow* and select **OK**.

l) Observe that qryReorderNow appears in the queries section of the navigation pane.

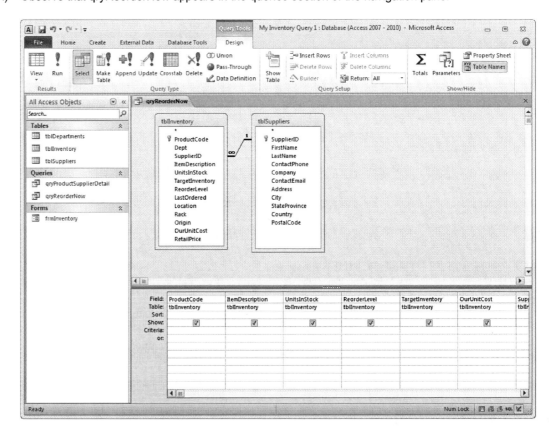

2. Run and save the query.

   a) Select **Design→Results→Run** to run the query. The query results show inventory data joined with supplier data.

   b) Observe the number of records in the results. The query results in 49 records.

   c) Open the tblInventory table.

   d) Observe the number of records in the tblInventory table. There are 49 records in tblInventory, so all 49 of the records in tblInventory were shown by the qryReorderNow query. At this point, the query essentially just creates a new view that displays all records in tblInventory, joining fields from tblSuppliers into that view.

3. Close tblInventory.

4. Save the database.

TOPIC B

Sort and Filter Data in a Query

Access queries can sort and filter results that are displayed, saving you the extra step of sorting the results manually.

Query Criteria

You can provide *query criteria* to specify which records should be included in a query result. You provide query criteria by writing a mathematical or logical *expression* that produces a result. You can include one or many criteria in a query.

ProductCode	ItemDescription	UnitsInStock	TargetInventory	ReorderLevel
bathhw-2	Windsor Model 24" Double Towel Bar Brushed Nickel	22	25	10
bathhw-3	Windsor Model 24" Single Towel Bar Brushed Nickel	18	25	10
bathhw-32	4 in. 2-Handle Low-Arc 4" Bathroom Faucet in Vibrant Brushed Nickel	5	25	10
bathhw-34	Antique 8 in. 2-Handle Low Arc Bathroom Faucet Polished Brass	6	25	10
bathhw-4	Edinburgh Model 24" Double Towel Bar Brass	12	25	10
bathhw-5	Edinburgh Model 24" Single Towel Bar Brass	14	25	10
bathhw-6	Albany Model 24" Double Towel Bar Plastic	15	25	10
bathhw-7	Albany Model 24" Single Towel Bar Plastic	8	25	10

UnitsInStock <= ReorderLevel

ProductCode	ItemDescription	UnitsInStock	TargetInventory	ReorderLevel
bathhw-32	4 in. 2-Handle Low-Arc 4" Bathroom Faucet in Vibrant Brushed Nickel	5	25	10
bathhw-34	Antique 8 in. 2-Handle Low Arc Bathroom Faucet Polished Brass	6	25	10
bathhw-7	Albany Model 24" Single Towel Bar Plastic	8	25	10

Figure 3–3: Query Criteria

Wildcards

Various *wildcard* characters can be used in conjunction with query criteria. Wildcards enable you to match records based on patterns, rather than requiring a literal character-by-character match. Include them where you would provide a value. They can be substituted for literal values, as shown in the following table.

Character	Substitutes For
*	Any number of characters. Can only appear at the beginning or the end of the string.
?	Any single alphabetical character. Can appear anywhere in a string.
[ ]	Any single character from those provided within brackets.
[!]	Any character other than those provided within brackets.
#	Any single numeric character. Can appear anywhere in a string.

Character	Substitutes For
[-]	Any single character from within the range provided in brackets.

Use the *like operator* within a query to search for records that contain values based on a search pattern or wildcards. A wildcard represents a character or group of characters that will be allowed for pattern matching.

Examples

Examples of using the like operator include:

- **Like "W*"** : All values that start with w, such as Wilson, Woodworker's, and Wheelhouse.
- **Like "*x*"** : All values that contain x, such oxygen, axe, and oxen.
- **Like "*x"**: All values that end with x, such as Unix and Linux.
- **Like "V[68]"** : Values of V6 or V8.
- **Like "V[!68]"** : Values whose first character is V but whose second character is not 6 or 8, such as V12 or V4.
- **Like "s?n"**: All values that start with s, end with n, and are three characters in length, such as sin, son, and sun.
- **Like "V#"** : All values that start with x and are two characters in length where the second character is a number, such as V8 and V6.

Comparison Operators

Comparison operators are used to compare two values and return a true or false result.

ProductCode	UnitsInStock	Operator	ReorderLevel	Result
bathhw-2	22	<=	10	False
bathhw-3	18	<=	10	False
bathhw-32	5	<=	10	True ←
bathhw-34	6	<=	10	True ←
bathhw-4	12	<=	10	False
bathhw-5	14	<=	10	False
bathhw-6	15	<=	10	False
bathhw-7	8	<=	10	True ←

Records with True result will be shown.

Figure 3-4: A comparison operator.

Comparison Operators

The following comparison operators are supported in Access for use in query comparisons.

Operator	Description	Example
=	Equals	value1 = value2

Operator	Description	Example
<	Is Less Than	value1 < value2
< =	Is Less Than or Equal To	value1 <= value 2
>	Is Greater Than	value1 > value2
> =	Is Greater Than or Equal To	value1 >= value2
< >	Is Not Equal To	value1 <> value2
Between ... And	Is Within a Range	value1 Between value2 And value3
Is Null	Has No Value	value1 Is Null

Logical Operators

Logical operators evaluate the result of one or more logical conditions and return a value of either true or false.

Suppose:

* Expression1 = False
* Expression2 = True

Operator	Description	Result
AND	True if both conditions are true	Expression1 And Expression2 returns False
OR	True if either condition is true	Expression1 Or Expression2 returns True
NOT	True if the condition is not true (Returns the opposite of the condition state)	Not Expression1 returns True

Figure 3-5: Logical operators.

Logical Operators Used in Access Queries

The following logical operators are supported in Access for use in query comparisons.

Operator	Description	Example
AND	True if both conditions are true.	Condition1 AND Condition2
OR	True if either condition is true.	Condition1 OR Condition2
NOT	True if the condition is not true.	NOT Condition1

Sorting

In a large table, it may be difficult to work with records if they are not displayed in a useful order. The default sort order returned from a table may not be the most useful order in which to return values. Fortunately, one of the tasks a query can perform is sorting query results. Fields can be sorted in ascending or descending order. An Access query can sort records based on multiple fields. This is called a *multi-level sort*. You apply a sort to multiple columns, and Access applies the sorts in order, essentially performing the sorts working from right to left. So, the sort column the farthest to the left is the primary sort. If there are multiple items in that column with the same value, that group will be sub-sorted by the next sort column to the right.

 Access the Checklist tile on your LogicalCHOICE course screen for reference information and job aids on How to Sort and Filter Table Data in a Query

ACTIVITY 3-3
Filtering a Query Using a Comparison Operator

Before You Begin
The My Inventory Query 1 database is open. The results of qryReorderNow are shown in a datasheet.

Scenario
You want to continue working on the query that will produce your weekly product order. You will filter the query to show all products where your inventory level is low.

1. Observe that there are 49 records in the result. All inventory items are shown in the current result.

2. Consider the following question.

    Which fields would enable you to determine which items need to be reordered?

3. Modify qryReorderNow to show only those items that currently need to be reordered from the supplier.
    a) Open qryReorderNow in **Design View**.
    b) As needed, adjust the size and location of the field lists and move the split bar so the query design grid is showing and field lists display all of the fields, as shown in the following graphic.

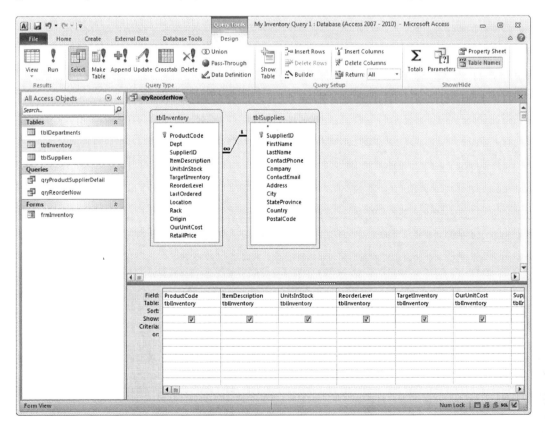

c) In the query design grid, in the **Criteria** row of the **UnitsInStock** field, type **<= re**. As you type, Access will provide a pop-up menu showing suggested values. **ReorderLevel** is one of the values shown.

d) Double-click **ReorderLevel**. Access completes the criteria statement for you, enclosing the **ReorderLevel** field name within brackets.

e) Save and run the query.

f) Observe the query results. The results have been filtered down to 27 records that match the criteria of *UnitsInStock <= ReorderLevel*. For each of the matching records, observe that the **UnitsInStock** value is less than or equal to the **ReorderLevel**.

g) Close the qryReorderNow query.

ACTIVITY 3-4
Filtering a Query Using a Wildcard

Before You Begin
The My Inventory Query 1 database is open. No objects are open in the document pane.

Scenario
Because prices for wood vary with the market, you decide you need a way to quickly view the prices for your woodworkers' project packs. These are packages of different varieties of wood that are small enough to ship inexpensively through the mail, but large enough to contain enough wood for a small woodworking project. Because you have consistently named all of your project packs with the pak- prefix, you decide you could use this as a query filter.

The qryReorderNow query already contains the fields you want to work with. You just need to have a different filter criterion to view product codes that begin with pak-. So you will modify a copy of qryReorderNow to create your new query.

---

1. Create a copy of qryReorderNow and remove its filter criterion.
    a) In the queries section of the navigation pane, select **qryReorderNow**.
    b) Select **Home→Clipboard→Copy**.
    c) Select **Home→Clipboard→Paste**. You are prompted to name the query you are pasting.
    d) In the **Query Name** text box, type *qryProjectPacks* and select **OK**. The query appears in the navigation pane.
    e) Open qryProjectPacks and display it in **Design View**.
    f) In the query design grid, select and delete the criteria for **UnitsInStock**.

2. Modify the qryProjectPacks query to show products with a **ProductCode** that begins with pak-.
    a) In the query design grid, in the **Criteria** row of the **ProductCode** field, type *like pak-**.
    b) Press **Enter**.

Access corrects your entry, capitalizing the like operator and enclosing **pak-*** within quotation marks.
    c) Run qryProjectPacks and observe the results.

ProductCode	ItemDescription	UnitsInStock	ReorderLevel
pak-ashwt-24	Project Pack - 24 Board Feet 3/4" Select White Ash	3	5
pak-baswd-25	Project Pack - 25 Board Feet 3/4" Select Basswood	10	5
pak-btrnt-25	Project Pack - 25 Board Feet 3/4" Select Butternut	12	5
pak-chrbk-25	Project Pack - 25 Board Feet 3/4" Select Black Cherry	6	5
pak-mplhd-23	Project Pack - 23 Board Feet 3/4" Select Hard Maple	40	5
pak-mplrd-25	Project Pack - 25 Board Feet 3/4" Select Red Maple	15	5
pak-oakrd-23	Project Pack - 23 Board Feet 3/4" Select Red Oak	23	5
pak-oakwq-23	Project Pack - 23 Board Feet 3/4" Select Quartersawn White Oak	12	5
pak-oakwt-23	Project Pack - 23 Board Feet 3/4" Select White Oak	22	5
pak-poptu-25	Project Pack - 25 Board Feet 3/4" Tulip Poplar	23	5
pak-walbk-25	Project Pack - 25 Board Feet 3/4" Black Walnut	12	5

11 project pack records are shown.

d) Save the database.

e) Close the qryProjectPacks query.

The Zoom Dialog Box

Use the **Zoom** dialog box to view and edit expressions that are too long to view completely within the query design grid. Display an expression in the **Zoom** dialog box by right-clicking the field and selecting **Zoom**.

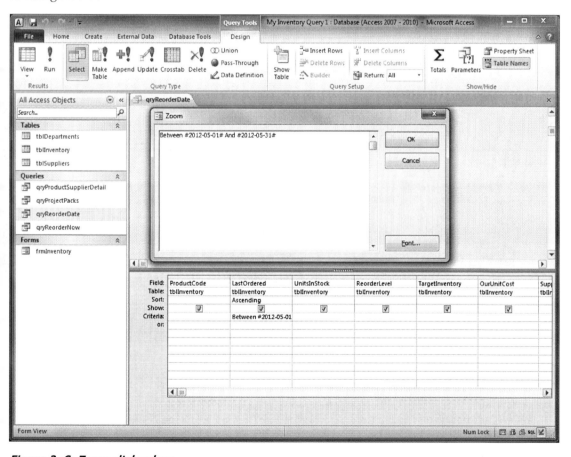

Figure 3-6: Zoom dialog box.

ACTIVITY 3-5
Filtering a Query Using a Date Range

Before You Begin

The My Inventory Query 1 database is open. No objects are open in the document pane.

Scenario

When you place an order, you indicate the last order date in the record for each product ordered. This enables you to monitor how frequently you can order certain products. You decide it would be helpful to have a query that pulls up a list of products last ordered within a certain date range. You will make a copy of qryReorderNow and use it as the basis for this new query.

1. Create a copy of qryReorderNow, naming it *qryReorderDate*

2. In qryReorderDate, create a query condition to show the last order date for each product.
   a) Display qryReorderDate in **Design View**.
   b) Remove the filter criterion in the **UnitsInStock** column.
   c) Observe the columns in the query design grid, scrolling horizontally as needed. The **LastOrdered** column is not present in the query design.
   d) In the **tblInventory** field list, double-click **LastOrdered**. The column is appended to the right of the other columns. Depending on where you had previously scrolled the query design grid, you may need to scroll right to see the new **LastOrdered** column.

3. Rearrange the **LastOrdered** field to appear between **ItemDescription** and **UnitsInStock**.
   a) Select the top border of the **LastOrdered** column to select the column.
   b) Drag the top border of the **LastOrdered** column to the left and release when it is positioned between **ItemDescription** and **UnitsInStock**. As you move to the left, the grid automatically scrolls in the same direction.

Field:	ProductCode	ItemDescription	LastOrdered	UnitsInStock	ReorderLevel
Table:	tblInventory	tblInventory	tblInventory	tblInventory	tblInventory
Sort:					
Show:	☑	☑	☑	☑	☑
Criteria:					
or:					

4. Add a filter to show only items last ordered during the month of May 2012.
   a) In the query design grid, in the **Criteria** row of the **LastOrdered** field, type *between 5/1/2012 and 5/31/2012*
   b) Press **Enter**. You probably cannot see the entire criterion you entered within the narrow field.
   c) Right-click the criterion you just entered, and select **Zoom** to see the entire expression. Access reformatted what you entered to *Between #5/1/2012# And #5/31/2012#*

Note: Depending on how dates are configured on your system, your date format may be slightly different from what is shown here.

d) Select **OK** to close the **Zoom** dialog box.

e) Run the query and observe the results. Thirty-two products were ordered in May 2012. The products are not sorted by date.

5. Modify qryReorder to sort by **LastOrderedDate**.

a) Display qryReorderDate in **Design View**.

b) In the query design grid, in the **LastOrdered** column, select the **Sort** row to display a drop-down arrow.

c) Select the box arrow to display a list of sort options.

d) Select **Ascending**.

6. Run the query and observe the results. The products are now sorted by **LastOrdered** date.

7. Save the database.

8. Close **qryReorderDate** and any other tabs that you may have open.

TOPIC C

Perform Calculations in a Query

At times, you may need to perform calculations based on dynamic values in your database. For example, as customers purchase products from your store, you would like to update the inventory count and determine whether the inventory is low enough to warrant a resupply of stock. By adding a calculated field that checks the difference between inventory and a reorder level, you can trigger a new order when inventory dips below the reorder level. Access can calculate values based on one or more fields and display the result in the query output.

Arithmetic Operators

Arithmetic operators perform mathematical calculations on values, returning a numeric result.

The following arithmetic operators are supported in Access.

Operator	Description	Example
+	Adds two values.	10 + 2 returns 12
-	Subtracts the second value from the first value.	10 - 2 returns 8
*	Multiplies two values.	10 * 2 returns 20
/	Divides the first value by the second value.	10 / 2 returns 5
^	Multiplies the first value exponentially by the second value.	10 ^ 2 returns 100

 Access the Checklist tile on your LogicalCHOICE course screen for reference information and job aids on How to Perform Calculations

ACTIVITY 3-6
Performing Calculations in a Query

Before You Begin

The My Inventory Query 1 database is open. No objects are open in the document pane.

Scenario

You have developed a query to provide you with a list of products that need to be ordered because your inventory on those products is low. Now you want to calculate the total price of the order. You'll need to calculate how many of each item you need to order. Then you'll calculate the total cost. You'll program the query to do this for you.

---

1. Determine how to calculate order amounts for each item.
   a) Open qryReorderNow in **Design View**.
   b) Observe the design of the query. This query joins data from tblInventory and tblSuppliers. It filters to show only those records where **UnitsInStock** are less than or equal to **ReorderLevel**.
   c) Run the query and observe the results. Only items that need to be reordered are listed.

2. Consider the following question.

   How might you determine *how many* of each item you need to order?

3. Add a column to show the order quantity for each item.
   a) Display qryReorderNow in **Design View**.
   b) In the query design grid, right-click in the blank **Field** row after the **LastName** column.

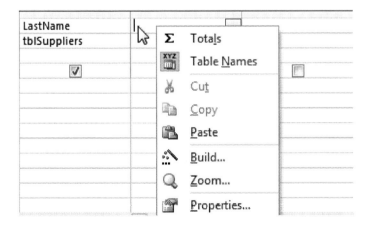

   c) Select **Build** to open the **Expression Builder**.

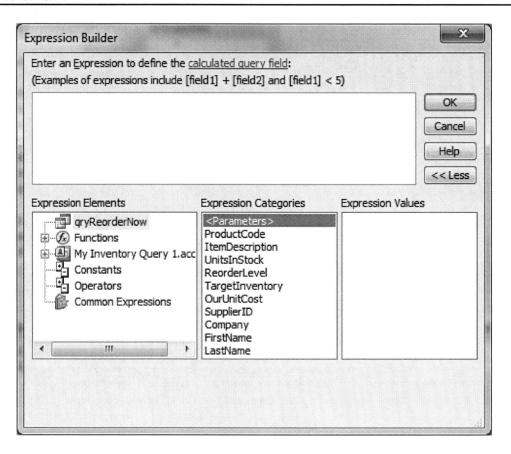

d) In the **Expression Elements** list box, select **qryReorderNow**. Fields and other expression categories that are available in the query you selected are listed in **Expression Categories**.

e) In the **Expression Categories** list box, double-click **TargetInventory** to add it to the **Expression** text box, and observe that it is enclosed in brackets. As you can see, you can use the lists at the bottom of the **Expression Builder** to help you add various elements to your expression.

f) Type **-** to add the minus operator to your expression. You could have selected it from the **Operators** list under **Expression Elements**; but in this case, it was easier to just type it. When using the **Expression Builder**, you can edit the expression directly as well as pick elements from the lists.

g) Type *units* and press **Enter**. Access determined the next thing you would type based on what you already typed, and it filled in the remainder of the expression value for you when you pressed **Enter**.

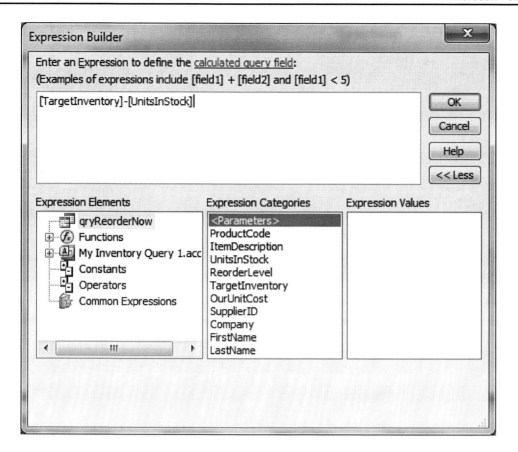

h) Select **OK** to close the **Expression Builder** dialog box.
i) Save the database and run the query.
j) Observe the results. The calculated field appears on the far right, and is named **Expr1**. It shows the number of items the need to be ordered to replenish each item to target inventory levels.

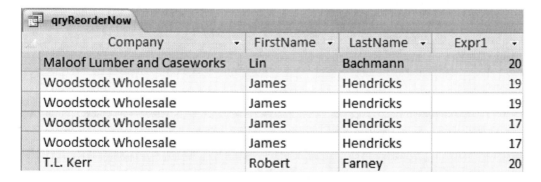

Company	FirstName	LastName	Expr1
Maloof Lumber and Caseworks	Lin	Bachmann	20
Woodstock Wholesale	James	Hendricks	19
Woodstock Wholesale	James	Hendricks	19
Woodstock Wholesale	James	Hendricks	17
Woodstock Wholesale	James	Hendricks	17
T.L. Kerr	Robert	Farney	20

4. Rename the calculated field and position it between **TargetInventory** and **OurUnitCost**.
   a) Switch qryReorderNow to **Design View**.
   b) Right-click the **Expr1** field title and select **Zoom**. The **Zoom** dialog box shows the field title in a larger text box for easy editing. Since you didn't provide a name for the calculated field, Access provided one for you. You can change it to something more meaningful.
   c) Change **Expr1** to *OrderQty*. There is no existing table field by this name. You are creating a temporary calculated field "on the fly."

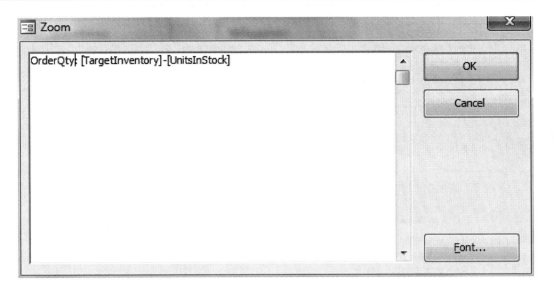

d) Select **OK** to close the **Zoom** dialog box.
e) Observe the location of the **OrderQty** calculated field. You will move it between **TargetInventory** and **OurUnitCost**.
f) Select the top border of the **OrderQty** column to select the column.
g) Drag the top border of the **OrderQty** column to the left and release when you have moved the column between **TargetInventory** and **OurUnitCost**. The query grid will automatically scroll as you drag towards the left.

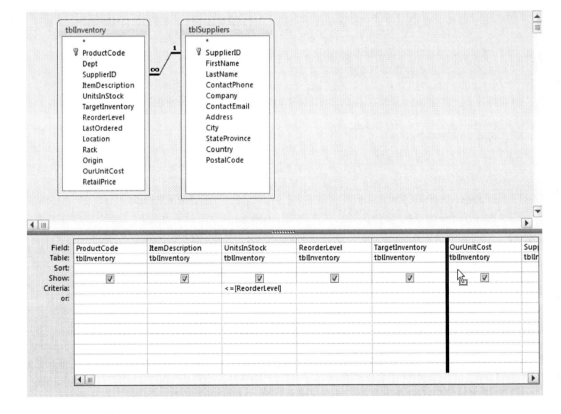

ProductCode	ItemDescription	UnitsInStock	ReorderLevel	TargetInventory	OrderQty: [TargetInve	Our
tblInventory	tblInventory	tblInventory	tblInventory	tblInventory		tblIr
☑	☑	☑	☑	☑	☑	
		<=[ReorderLevel]				

h) Save the database and run the query.

5. Add a new calculated field that will multiply **OrderQty** by **OurUnitCost** to determine the cost of the order for that item. Name the field *OrderCost*. **OrderCost** should appear between **OurUnitCost** and **SupplierID**. Save the database and test the query.

6. Close the database.

Summary

In this lesson, you learned to use queries to create reusable instructions to perform complex operations on dynamic table data, including joining data from multiple tables, sorting and filtering, and performing calculations.

What are the differences between using the Query Wizard to build a query versus building a query directly in the Design View?

What are benefits of using the Expression Builder?

 Note: Check your LogicalCHOICE Course screen for opportunities to interact with your classmates, peers, and the larger LogicalCHOICE online community about the topics covered in this course or other topics you are interested in. From the Course screen you can also access available resources for a more continuous learning experience.

 Note: Access the LearnTO **View SQL, the Language Behind the Query** presentation from the **LearnTO** tile on the LogicalCHOICE Course screen.

4 | Creating Advanced Queries

Lesson Time: 1 hour

Lesson Objectives

In this lesson, you will create advanced queries. You will:

- Create a parameter query.

- Create an action query.

- Create an unmatched or duplicate query.

- Create a PivotTable or PivotChart.

Lesson Introduction

One benefit of queries is that they make complex data management tasks repeatable. As your database content changes over time, you can rely on saved queries to perform the same set of operations on your data each time you run them. But suppose your needs change slightly each time you run a query. One time you might want to see products from Vendor A, another time those from Vendor B. In this lesson, you will create flexible queries that you can instantly tailor to your needs at the moment you them.

Up to this point, you may have believed that queries are passive. You run the query, and it shows you a temporary view of results without actually changing the content stored in the database. Some queries work this way. But in this lesson, you will create queries that perform an action, such as deleting or modifying matching records. Such action queries can be a powerful tool for making mass updates to a database.

Finally, you will see how queries can roll up data into a special view called a PivotTable, that can help to reveal patterns within data that might not be evident in a normal database view. You will also create a graphic version of this, called a PivotChart.

TOPIC A

Create Parameter Queries

You may often find it necessary to make data retrieval interactive so that data is retrieved to meet the specific needs of users. In this topic, you will retrieve records based on input criteria. You may find that in some cases, it would be valuable if you could select records by entering values, which serve as a criteria at runtime. For example, users may need to retrieve all records which contain information pertaining to particular states in the United States. One possible way of recovering such information is by creating a separate query for each of the 50 states; however, a better approach would be to create one query that will ask users for the state in which they are interested. Doing this will save you development time and let you create a more concise database.

Parameter Queries

Parameter queries prompt the user for additional criteria before executing the query. This provides queries with greater flexibility and gives the user more control over the results. Parameter queries can prompt for multiple criteria, providing a separate prompt for each criterion. Access can display up to 50 characters in the prompt message. Characters such as periods, exclamation marks, and square brackets are not permitted with a prompt since these characters have special meaning in queries. The prompt message should not match the field name.

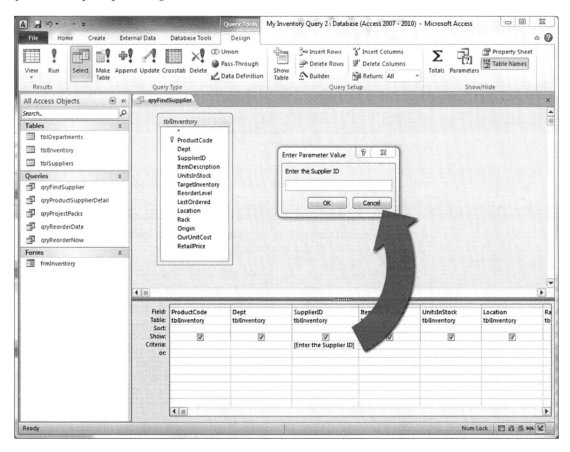

Figure 4-1: A parameter query displays a prompt.

Matching a Parameter Query

When you use a parameter query alone as a criterion, the search would be case-insensitive, but spelling must match exactly. With a query criterion of **[Enter the Supplier ID]**, the "Enter the Supplier ID" prompt is displayed.

Suppose the user enters "ogg" in the input box. In this example:

- **Ogg** would be a match.
- **ogg** would be a match.
- **ogg-32** would *not* be a match.
- **Froggy-12** would *not* be a match.

Wildcards and Parameter Queries

You can use the ampersand (&) operator to concatenate (join together) multiple values in a wildcard expression. For example, the following query criterion will prompt the user for a text value, and will find all records that have the text value anywhere within the target field. Without the wildcards appended to either side of the parameter value, only exact matches would be found.

Consider the following example:

Like "*" & [Enter the Supplier ID] & "*"

With this example, suppose the user enters "ogg" when the "Enter the Supplier ID" prompt is displayed.

- **Ogg** would be a match.
- **Froggy-12** would be a match.
- **64-ogg** would be a match.

The Ampersand Operator

Use the ampersand operator to join two character strings. The ampersand operator can be used in combination with the asterisk (*) wildcard to link more data to criteria specified by the user as part of a parameter query.

 Access the Checklist tile on your LogicalCHOICE course screen for reference information and job aids on How to Create and Run a Parameter Query

ACTIVITY 4-1
Creating a Parameter Query

Data Files

C:\091001Data\Creating Advanced Queries\Inventory Query 2.accdb

Scenario

You would like to be able to pull up a datasheet showing supplier IDs that match search text that you enter when you run the query. A parameter query is the way to accomplish this.

1. Open the C:\091001Data\Creating Advanced Queries\Inventory Query 2.accdb database. If a security prompt is shown, select **Enable Content**.

2. Save the database in C:\091001Data\Creating Advanced Queries as **My Inventory Query 2** and select **Enable Content** if you are prompted.

3. Create a new query to show an inventory list.
   a) Select **Create→Queries→Query Design**.
   b) Select **tblInventory** and select **Add**.
   c) Select **Close**.
   d) Double-click each of the following fields to add them from tblInventory into the query design grid. The fields will be arranged from left to right in the order that you add them:
      - ProductCode
      - Dept
      - SupplierID
      - ItemDescription
      - UnitsInStock
      - Location
      - Rack
      - LastOrdered

4. Add a criterion prompt in the **SupplierID** column.
   a) In the query design grid, in the **SupplierID** column and in the **Criteria** row, type *[Enter the Supplier ID]*
   b) Save the database. You are prompted to save the new query.
   c) Name the query *qryFindSupplier* and select **OK**.

5. Run the query and enter the **SupplierID** criterion.
   a) Run the query.
   b) Type *woodstock* and select **OK**.
   c) Observe the resulting records. All of the products for WOODSTOCK are shown. It does not matter that you entered the criterion in lowercase.

6. Run the query again with a different criterion.
   a) Select **Home→Records→Refresh All**. You are prompted to enter a new supplier ID.
   b) Type *wood* and select **OK**.

c) Observe that there are no matching records. Partial text is not matched with your current query. You need to use wildcards to provide that sort of flexibility in the search parameter.

Access the Checklist tile on your LogicalCHOICE course screen for reference information and job aids on How to Use Wildcards within a Query

ACTIVITY 4–2
Using Wildcards in a Parameter Query

Before You Begin

The My Inventory Query 2 database is open, and qryFindSupplier is displayed in **Datasheet** view.

Scenario

You will modify the existing qryFindSupplier query so partial string matches will be included in the query result.

---

1. Examine qryFindSupplier in **Design View**.
   a) Display qryFindSupplier in **Design View**.
   b) Observe the criterion for **SupplierID**. Currently, the query will find exactly the text that the user enters. If the user enters a partial **SupplierID**, the records will not be found.

2. Add a wildcard to the query to find the text anywhere within the field.
   a) Right-click the **Criteria** for **SupplierID** and select **Zoom**.
   b) Change the criterion for **SupplierID** to *Like "*" & [Enter the Supplier ID] & "*"* and select **OK**.

   c) Save and run the query.
   d) Type *wood* and select **OK**.
   e) Observe the results. Products supplied by WOODSTOCK are listed.
   f) Select **Home→Records→Refresh All**.
   g) Type *k* and select **OK**.
   h) Observe the results. Records containing a **k** anywhere in the **SupplierID** are shown.

3. Save the database and close **qryFindSupplier**.

ACTIVITY 4–3
Creating a Query with Multiple Parameters

Before You Begin
The My Inventory Query 2 database is open, and no objects are currently open in the documents pane.

Scenario
You currently have a query that searches a range between two dates. The dates are hard-coded in the query. You will modify the query to prompt for the date range at the moment the query is run. This means you will need to create a parameter query with two prompts, the start date and the end date.

---

1. Change the qryReorderDate query to prompt for a date range.
   a) Run the qryReorderDate query and observe the results. Only items that were last ordered in May 2012 are listed.
   b) Display qryReorderDate in **Design View**.
   c) Right-click the **Criteria** for **LastOrdered** and select **Zoom**.
   d) Observe the query design. The query is hard-coded to a specified date range.
   e) Change the criterion for the **LastOrdered** field to *Between [Enter Start Date] And [Enter End Date]*
   f) Select **OK**.
   g) Save the database and run the query. The first prompt is shown.

   h) Type *6/1/2012* and select **OK**. The second prompt is shown.

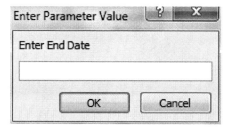

   i) Type *6/30/2012* and select **OK**.
   j) Observe the results. Items ordered in June 2012 are shown.

2. Close all open tabs.

TOPIC B

Create Action Queries

Typically, the changes you make to a database are small—one record at a time. Sometimes, however, you may need to make a mass update to multiple records based on a pattern. For example, you might choose to increase prices for all products within a certain product line. An action query can automate such tasks for you.

Action Queries

The simplest form of a query is sometimes called a *select query*, in contrast to an *action query*, which enables you to move, append, update, or delete matching records within a table. Whereas a select query is oriented toward displaying data, an action query is oriented toward updating data. Action queries can be useful for making data modifications on a large scale. Because an action query cannot be undone, you should back up your database or affected tables before you run an action query so you can restore the data if you are not satisfied with the results. Note that you can preview matching records in **Design** view before executing an action query to see which records will be changed before you actually commit the change.

Types of Action Queries

Types of action queries are listed in the following table.

Action Type	Description
Append query	Adds records to a table.
Update query	Changes field values in a table.
Delete query	Deletes records that match criteria.
Make table query	Creates a new table to contain the query result.

Update Query Example

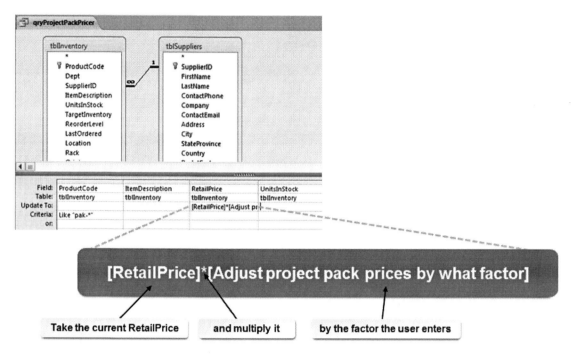

Figure 4-2: An action query update expression.

The example displayed shows an expression that would be entered in an update query. When you change the query type from a normal select query to an update query, a new row, **Update To**, is added in the query design grid. The expression you enter into this row calculates a result. When the update query runs, the result of that calculation becomes the new value for the field in which the **Update To** expression was placed.

> **Access the Checklist tile on your LogicalCHOICE course screen for reference information and job aids on How to Create Action Queries**

ACTIVITY 4-4
Creating Action Queries

Before You Begin
The My Inventory Query 2 database is open, and no objects are currently open in the documents pane.

Scenario
Rather than individually update the prices of your woodworker project packs, you have decided to create an action query that will find any product with a **ProductCode** that begins with **pak-** and adjust its price of by a factor that you enter when you run the query. So it will be a parameter query (to display a prompt for a price adjustment), and because it will make a modification to existing records, it will also be an action query.

Because you cannot undo an action query, you will first back up the table you are going to modify. And because qryProjectPacks already filters to show just the records with a **ProductCode** of **pak-**, you will use a copy of that query to create your action query.

1. Create a backup copy of tblInventory.
   a) In the **Tables** section of the navigation pane, select (but do not open) **tblInventory**.
   b) Select **Home→Clipboard→Copy**.
   c) Select **Home→Clipboard→Paste**. You are prompted to name the new table you are pasting.
   d) Change **Copy Of tblInventory** to *tblOldInventoryBackup* and select **OK**. You will copy both the table structure and data so you have a complete backup.

2. Create a new query based on qryProjectPacks.
   a) In the **Queries** section of the navigation pane, select the **qryProjectPacks** query.
   b) Select **Home→Clipboard→Copy**.
   c) Select **Home→Clipboard→Paste**. You are prompted to name the new query.
   d) Change **Copy Of qryProjectPacks** to *qryProjectPackPricer* and select **OK**.
   e) Run the qryProjectPackPricer and observe the results. Like the qryProjectPacks query from which it was copied, at this point, the only thing the query does is filter the inventory records to show only Project Packs.

ProductCode	ItemDescription	RetailPrice
pak-ashwt-24	Project Pack - 24 Board Feet 3/4" Select White Ash	$105.60
pak-baswd-25	Project Pack - 25 Board Feet 3/4" Select Basswood	$85.80
pak-btrnt-25	Project Pack - 25 Board Feet 3/4" Select Butternut	$123.20
pak-chrbk-25	Project Pack - 25 Board Feet 3/4" Select Black Cherry	$168.30
pak-mplhd-23	Project Pack - 23 Board Feet 3/4" Select Hard Maple	$115.50
pak-mplrd-25	Project Pack - 25 Board Feet 3/4" Select Red Maple	$100.10
pak-oakrd-23	Project Pack - 23 Board Feet 3/4" Select Red Oak	$107.80
pak-oakwq-23	Project Pack - 23 Board Feet 3/4" Select Quartersawn White Oak	$136.40
pak-oakwt-23	Project Pack - 23 Board Feet 3/4" Select White Oak	$107.80
pak-poptu-25	Project Pack - 25 Board Feet 3/4" Tulip Poplar	$85.80
pak-walbk-25	Project Pack - 25 Board Feet 3/4" Black Walnut	$167.20

f) Note the current prices the Project Packs. You can verify later that your price updater is working correctly by comparing against these prices.

g) Display qryProjectPackPricer in **Design View**.

3. Change the select query to an update query.

a) Select **Design→Query Type→Update**.

b) Observe that the **Select** icon is no longer selected within the **Design→Query Type** ribbon group. **Update** is now selected, and the **Update To** row has been added to the query design grid.

c) In the query design grid, in the **RetailPrice** column, in the **Update To** row, type *[RetailPrice]*[Adjust project pack prices by what factor]*

 Note: You may find it helpful to right-click the **Update To** cell in the **RetailPrice** column and select **Zoom** before you enter the expression.

d) Observe the expression you just entered. It prompts for a price update factor, which it multiplies by the current RetailPrice to produce a new price.

e) Save the database and run the query. You are prompted to enter the price update factor.

f) Type *1.02* and select **OK**. You will raise prices by 2% (1.02 times the current price).

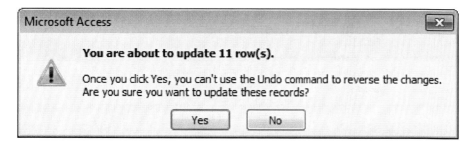

Microsoft Access

You are about to update 11 row(s).

Once you click Yes, you can't use the Undo command to reverse the changes.
Are you sure you want to update these records?

[Yes]   [No]

You created a backup table since the **Undo** command is unable to reverse an action query.

g) Select **Yes**.

h) Run the qryProjectPacks query to view all project packs.

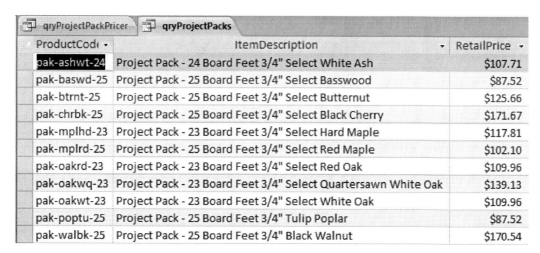

ProductCode	ItemDescription	RetailPrice
pak-ashwt-24	Project Pack - 24 Board Feet 3/4" Select White Ash	$107.71
pak-baswd-25	Project Pack - 25 Board Feet 3/4" Select Basswood	$87.52
pak-btrnt-25	Project Pack - 25 Board Feet 3/4" Select Butternut	$125.66
pak-chrbk-25	Project Pack - 25 Board Feet 3/4" Select Black Cherry	$171.67
pak-mplhd-23	Project Pack - 23 Board Feet 3/4" Select Hard Maple	$117.81
pak-mplrd-25	Project Pack - 25 Board Feet 3/4" Select Red Maple	$102.10
pak-oakrd-23	Project Pack - 23 Board Feet 3/4" Select Red Oak	$109.96
pak-oakwq-23	Project Pack - 23 Board Feet 3/4" Select Quartersawn White Oak	$139.13
pak-oakwt-23	Project Pack - 23 Board Feet 3/4" Select White Oak	$109.96
pak-poptu-25	Project Pack - 25 Board Feet 3/4" Tulip Poplar	$87.52
pak-walbk-25	Project Pack - 25 Board Feet 3/4" Black Walnut	$170.54

i) Observe the updated prices of the Project Packs.

4. Save the database.

5. Close qryProjectPacks and qryProjectPackPricer.

TOPIC C

Create Unmatched and Duplicate Queries

Part of the process of managing a database is simply keeping the database clean and efficient. In a large database, it is easy to end up with orphaned records over time—table entries that are no longer used or needed anywhere but are still in the database. Similarly, it is possible to end up with duplicated records. For example, you might have two different product codes (and separate records) representing the same product. There are two types of action queries, unmatched and duplicate, that can help you automate the process of finding and correcting such problems.

The Find Unmatched Query Wizard

The **Find Unmatched Query Wizard** finds records in a table or query that have no related records in another table or query. This can help you find unused records that can be deleted or archived.

The Find Duplicates Query Wizard

The **Find Duplicates Query Wizard** enables you to find records that have duplicate field values within a table or query. This can help you find records that have been inadvertently duplicated.

 Access the Checklist tile on your LogicalCHOICE course screen for reference information and job aids on How to Create Unmatched and Duplicate Queries

ACTIVITY 4-5
Creating Queries to Search for Unmatched and Duplicate Records

Before You Begin

The My Inventory Query 2 database is open, and no objects are currently open in the documents pane.

Scenario

You have some suppliers from whom you stopped purchasing products a while ago. You want to prune down the records in tblSuppliers by removing any suppliers that have no products listed in tblInventory.

You also suspect you have some duplicate records for products in your inventory table. You will use a query to eliminate the extra entries.

---

1. Create a query to find suppliers in tblSuppliers that are not referenced in tblInventory.
   a) Select **Create→Queries→Query Wizard** to open the **New Query** dialog box.
   b) In the **New Query** dialog box, select **Find Unmatched Query Wizard** and select **OK**.
   c) Select **Table: tblSuppliers.**

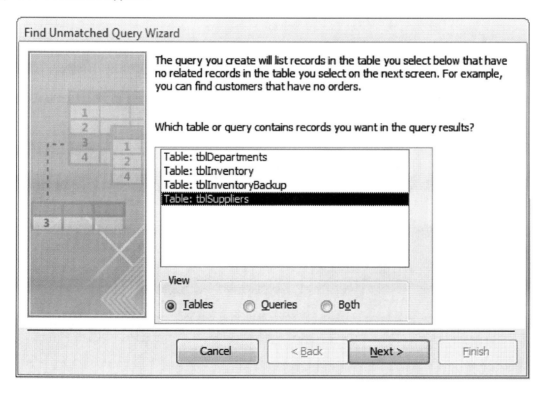

   d) Select **Next**.
   e) Select **Table: tblInventory.**

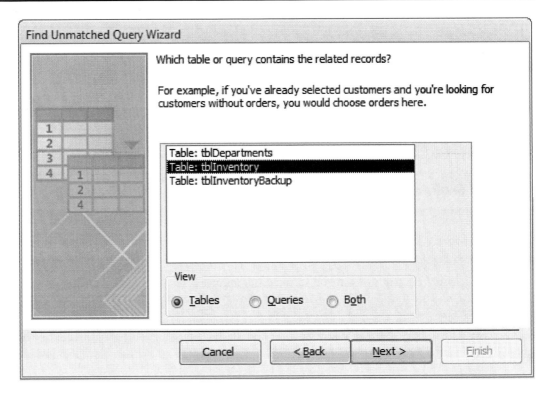

f) Select **Next**.
g) Observe that the **SupplierID** field is already matched as the default, so you do not need to change anything.

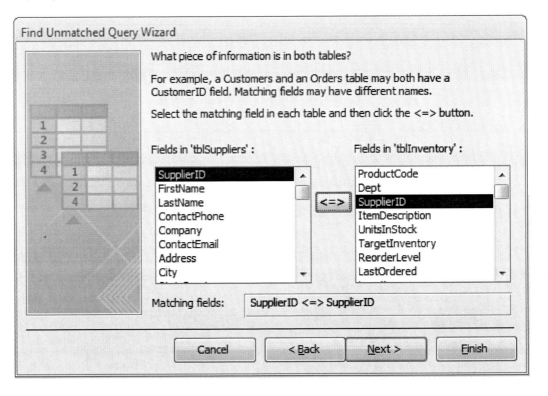

h) Select **Next**.
i) Select the **>>** button to show all fields in the query results.

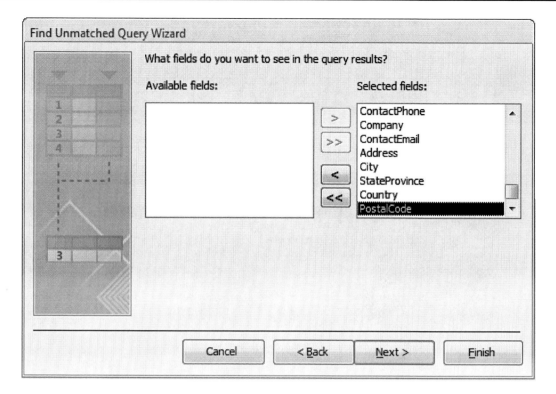

j) Select **Next**.
k) Change **tblSuppliers Without Matching tblInventory** to *qryUnusedSuppliers*

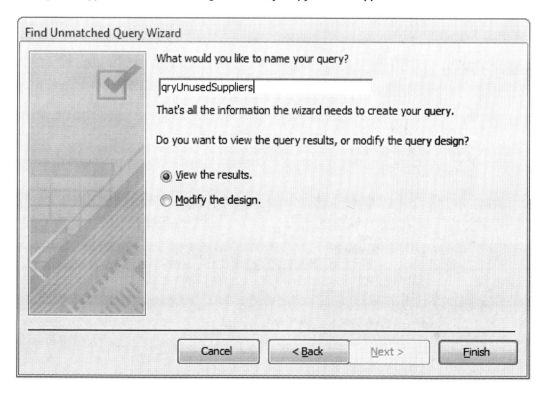

l) Select **Finish**.
m) Observe that seven vendors are not currently associated with products in tblInventory. You won't do so now, but if you wanted to, at this point you could delete some or all of these records.
n) Close the qryUnusedSuppliers query.

2. Create a query to find products that have multiple entries in tblInventory.

a) Select **Create→Queries→Query Wizard** to open the **New Query** dialog box.
b) In the **New Query** dialog box, select **Find Duplicates Query Wizard** and select **OK**.
c) Select **Table: tblInventory**.

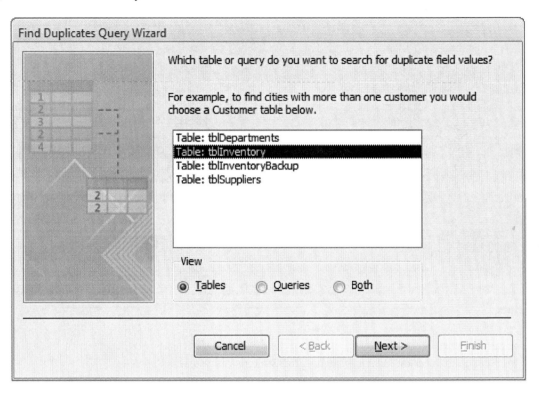

d) Select **Next**.
e) Select **ItemDescription** and select **>**. You will look for records that have duplicate information in the **ItemDescription** field.

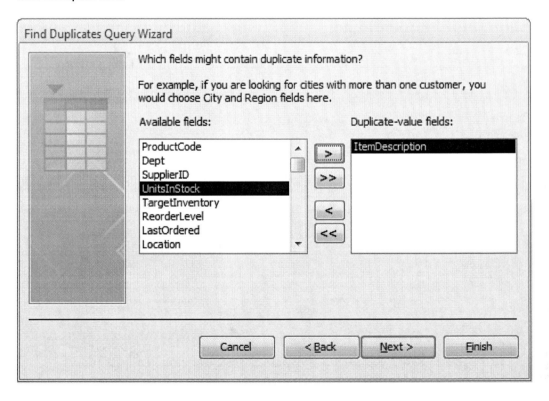

f) Select **Next**.

g) Select the **>>** button to show all fields in the query results.

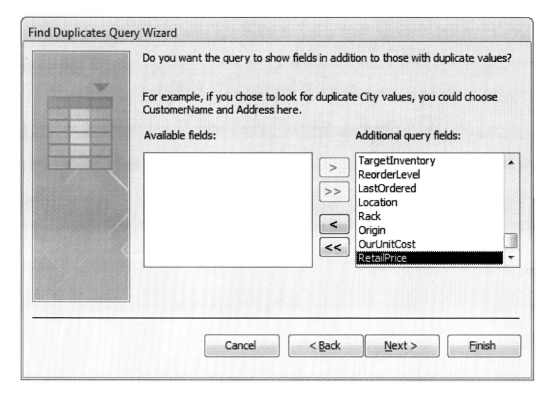

h) Select **Next**.

i) Change **Find duplicates for tblInventory** to *qryDuplicateProducts*

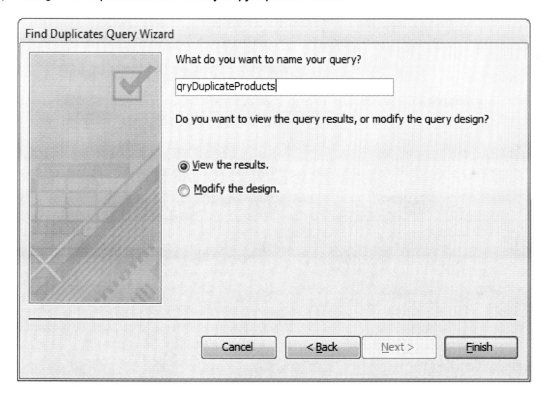

j) Select **Finish**.

k) Observe the three duplicates. The hinge-15 and hinge-25 records are extras. The hinge-12 record is the only one you want to keep.
l) Delete the records for hinge-15 and hinge-25. When you are prompted to confirm deletion, click **Yes**.
m) Close qryDuplicateProducts.

TOPIC D

Summarize Data

PivotTables and PivotCharts display data in a way that may provide insights that are not readily apparent through a direct display of table data.

Crosstab Queries

A *crosstab query* displays data grouped by category to summarize results or reveal patterns in categories of data. Unlike a select query, which lists values below the field name, a crosstab query displays the values of a field as a row heading, column heading, or in the cell intersection of the row and column. The name "crosstab" derives from "cross tabulation," and refers to the way values are distributed across the table, with categories labeled along the left and top. Values are placed where the column and row of the two category values intersect.

PivotTables

A *PivotTable* provides a view of data summarized by category. PivotTables group values in rows and columns, and can provide a calculated value (such as sum, average, and record count) at the intersection of each row and column.

	Origin ▼								
	Brazil	Canada	China	Germany	India	Mexico	UK	USA	Grand Total
	+|−	+|−	+|−	+|−	+|−	+|−	+|−	+|−	+|−
SupplierID ▼	# Products	# Products	# Products	# Products	# Products	# Products	# Products	# Products	# Products
ARBORHARVEST								1	1
ARTURO								3	3
GREENE								1	1
KER	2	3			4				9
LIMBERT								1	1
MALOOF			1						1
NAKASHIMA								3	3
NORMS								1	1
PUGG			9	1		2	1	2	15
UNDERHILL								1	1
WOODSTOCK			7			1		5	13
Grand Total	2	3	17	1	4	3	1	18	49

Figure 4–3: A PivotTable.

In this example, you can look up the number of products from **PUGG** that come from **Germany** by finding the intersection of the two values. In this case, there is one German PUGG product.

PivotCharts

A *PivotChart* displays PivotTable data in graphical format. PivotCharts can facilitate quick analysis of trends in data, in some cases more dramatically than a PivotTable.

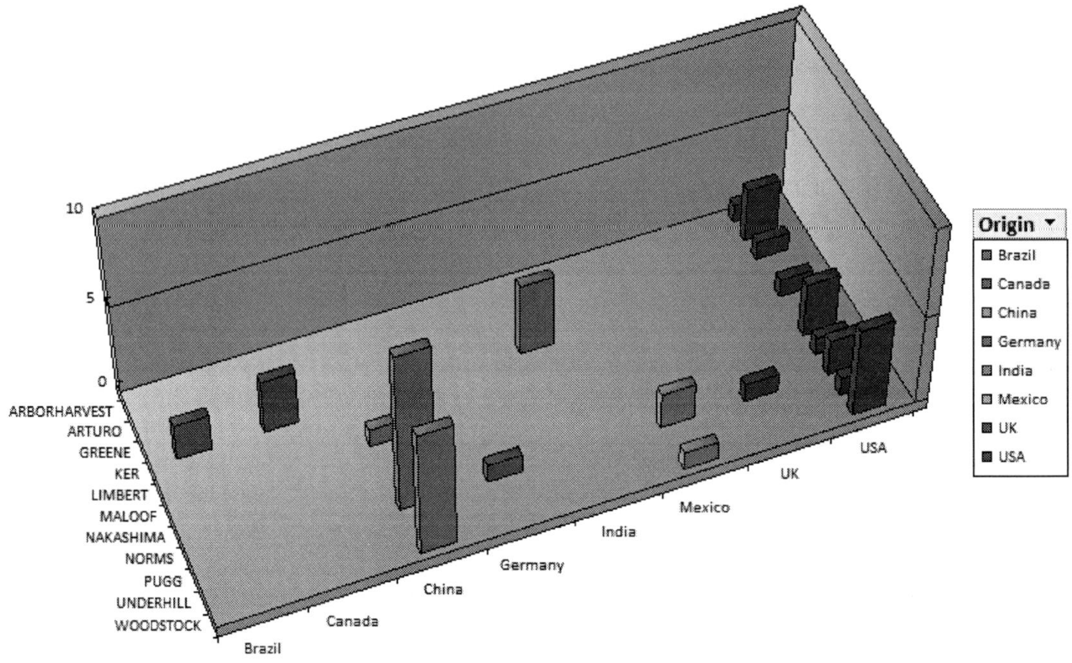

Figure 4-4: A PivotChart.

 Access the Checklist tile on your LogicalCHOICE course screen for reference information and job aids on How to Summarize Data

ACTIVITY 4-6
Creating a PivotTable

Before You Begin
The My Inventory Query 2 database is open, and no objects are currently open in the documents pane.

Scenario
You would like to analyze products from your various suppliers to get a sense of where their products are manufactured. You will create a PivotTable as shown here, with suppliers listed along the left side of the table, the countries of origin listed along the topic of the table, and product counts in each cell intersection.

	Country 1	Country 2	Country 3
Supplier 1	How many products Supplier 1 obtains from Country 1	How many products Supplier 1 obtains from Country 2	How many products Supplier 1 obtains from Country 3
Supplier 2	How many products Supplier 2 obtains from Country 1	How many products Supplier 2 obtains from Country 2	How many products Supplier 2 obtains from Country 3
Supplier 3	How many products Supplier 3 obtains from Country 1	How many products Supplier 3 obtains from Country 2	How many products Supplier 3 obtains from Country 3

1. Format a PivotTable query.
   a) Select **Create→Queries→Query Design**.
   b) Select **tblInventory** and select **Add**.
   c) Select **Close**.
   d) Double-click the following fields to add them to the query design grid:
      - **Origin**
      - **SupplierID**
      - **ProductCode**
   e) Save the database and name the query *qryOrigin* when you are prompted.
   f) Right-click the **qryOrigin** tab and select **PivotTable View**.
   g) From the **PivotTable Field** list, drag **Origin** to the **Drop Column Fields Here** area.

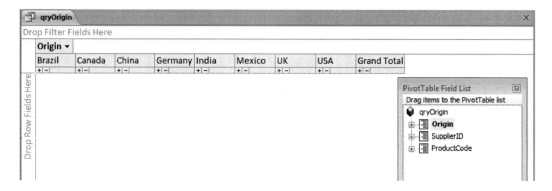

h) From the **PivotTable Field** list, drag **SupplierID** to the **Drop Row Fields Here** area.

i) From the **PivotTable Field** list, drag **ProductCode** to the **Drop Totals or Detail Fields Here** area.

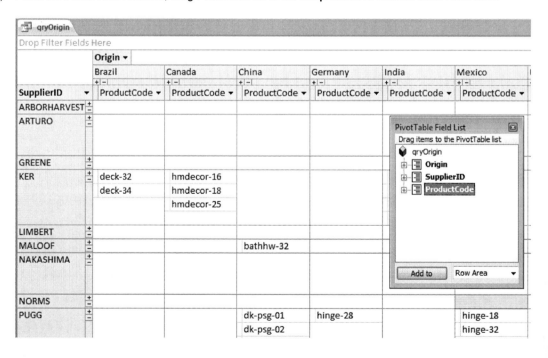

j) Observe the details shown in the query results. Each product that matches the row and column criteria is listed. For example, at the intersection of **KER** and **Canada** is listed hmdecor-16, hmdecor-18, and hmdecor-25. These are the Canadian products purchased from the KER supplier.

k) Save the database.

2. Format the PivotTable.

a) Select one of the **ProductCode** headings and select **Auto-Calc→Count**. The number of items in each intersection is shown, but the chart is getting quite busy with information.

b) Select one of the **ProductCode** headings and select **Hide Details**. Details are no longer shown. Only the counts are shown.

c) Select one of the **Count of ProductCode** headings and select **Property Sheet**. Select the **Captions** tab. Change **Caption** to *# Products* and close the **Properties** pane.

3. Format a pivot chart query.

a) Right-click the **qryOrigin** tab and select **PivotChart View**. The table is now shown as a chart.

b) Select **PivotChart Tools→Design→Show/Hide→Legend**.

c) Click within the chart to select it. A selection border appears around the chart when selected.

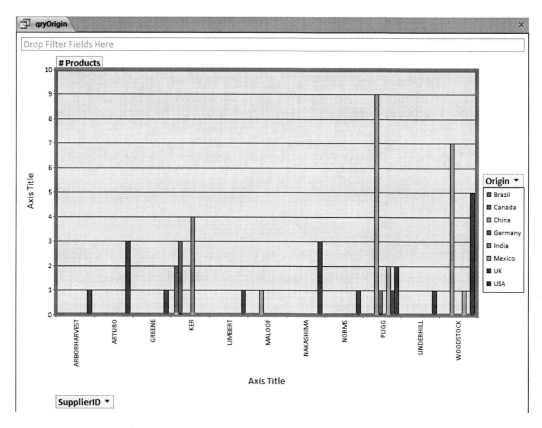

d) Select **PivotChart Tools→Design→Type→Change Chart Type**. Various chart types are shown.

e) Select various chart types until you find one you like. Experiment with other chart settings as well.

f) Close the **Properties** pane.

g) Save the database.

h) Close the database.

Summary

In this lesson, you learned how to create a parameter query to prompt the user for an input parameter when a query runs. You then constructed an action query to make a mass update to table values. You also created variations on a crosstab query, including a PivotTab and PivotChart.

What is the primary benefit of a crosstab query?

What is the difference between a PivotChart and a PivotTable?

Note: Check your LogicalCHOICE Course screen for opportunities to interact with your classmates, peers, and the larger LogicalCHOICE online community about the topics covered in this course or other topics you are interested in. From the Course screen you can also access available resources for a more continuous learning experience.

Note: Access the LearnTO **Manipulate Text Results in a Query** presentation from the **LearnTO** tile on the LogicalCHOICE Course screen.

5 | Generating Reports

Lesson Time: 1 hour, 10 minutes

Lesson Objectives

In this lesson, you will generate reports. You will:

- Create a report.

- Add a control to a report.

- Apply themes, fonts, and layout options to a report.

- Prepare a report to be printed.

Lesson Introduction

You created a database and have managed its content using a variety of tools provided by Microsoft® Office Access® 2010. For many, the ultimate reason to collect and organize data is to produce a report. In this lesson, you will create a report, add controls and change the report's layout, apply themes and layout options, and prepare a report to be printed.

TOPIC A

Create a Report

As your database starts to accumulate useful information, you may want to produce reports that you can use for analysis and subsequent publishing to print or digital form.

Report Creation Tools

You can create a report based on data in tables or from queries. Access 2010 includes a number of tools that help you create reports.

Tool	Description	Use When
Report	Create a report that includes all the fields in a table or query. The report will be displayed in the **Layout** view.	You would like to start with all fields from a certain table or query, then remove fields you don't want to use.
Blank Report	Add fields from tables and queries to create a report by displaying a blank report with necessary options. The report will be displayed in the **Layout** view. You can create the report by adding and positioning controls according to your requirements.	You would like to begin with no fields, and one-by-one add only those that you want.
Report Design	Create a new report or edit an existing one in the **Design** view. You can add fields from tables and queries. The report will be displayed in the **Layout** view.	You are building a new report based on an existing one.
Report Wizard	Create a report by adding fields from tables and queries. You can also group and sort the data in a report and customize the layout of a report.	You would like a wizard to guide you through steps to quickly create a new report with only the fields you require.

Report Object Views

The following are descriptions of the various views Access provides for creating and using reports.

View	Use This View To
Report	View data from a table or query in the layout defined by the report.
Print Preview	Examine how a report will appear when printed. Use options in the **Page Layout** group to configure print settings.
Design	Examine and change the structure of a report, including adding, removing, or modifying setting of controls to define how the report will appear.
Layout	Create or modify a report layout. This view presents data similar to the **Report** view, but enables you to change the report design, similar to the **Design** view. This view is optimized for making changes to the report's layout, such as resizing and rearranging report elements.

The Report Wizard

The *Report Wizard* guides you through steps to create a report based on one or more tables or queries, enabling you to select which fields you want to include in the report. The wizard also provides options to group and sort data, and to customize the layout of reports. However, there may be some options you want to use that the wizard doesn't provide. Once you have created a report, however, you can always make modifications to the report in **Design View**.

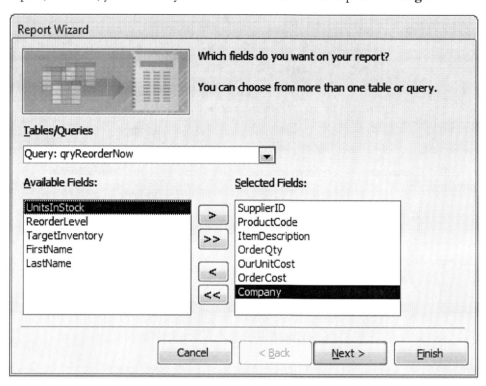

Figure 5-1: The Report Wizard.

 Access the Checklist tile on your LogicalCHOICE course screen for reference information and job aids on How to Create a Report

ACTIVITY 5-1
Creating Reports

Data Files

C:\091001Data\Generating Reports\Inventory Reporting.accdb

Scenario

As a "cheat sheet" for your employees to refer to when counting inventory, placing orders, and so forth, you periodically prepare an updated list of *all current department codes*. You will create a report to accomplish this directly from the inventory database.

---

1. Open the C:\091001Data\Generating Reports\Inventory Reporting.accdb database. Select **Enable Content** if you are prompted.

2. Save the database in C:\091001Data\Generating Reports as **My Inventory Reporting** and select **Enable Content** if you are prompted.

3. Consider the following question.

   What approach would you use to quickly create a report that lists all of the fields from the tblInventory table?

4. Generate a report.
   a) In the navigation pane, select **tblDepartments**.
   b) Select **Create→Reports→Report**. A report is generated from the table. Reports can also be generated directly from a query. All fields are included. When you create a report this way, Access makes assumptions about the fields and the layout, but you could revise the layout and remove fields if you desired.
   c) Save the database, naming the report *rptDepartments* when you are prompted.

5. Examine the various report views.
   a) Right-click the **rptDepartments** tab and select **Print Preview**. This view enables you to see the report as it will appear when printed and provides ribbon options related to printing. Page breaks are in effect, so you can see how many pages will be in the report when printed, and what each page will contain. The navigation bar at the bottom of the screen provides navigation buttons if the report contains more than one page.
   b) Right-click the **rptDepartments** tab and select **Layout View**. This view provides a preview of the report similar to **Print Preview**, but includes ribbon options for adjusting the layout and controls used in the report.
   c) Right-click the **rptDepartments** tab and select **Design View**. While **Print Preview** and **Layout View** are oriented toward showing the *graphical* design of the finished report, this view is optimized for adjusting the *logical* design of the report. For example, you can use this view to add and set properties of controls used in the report.
   d) Close rptDepartments and any other open database objects.

ACTIVITY 5-2
Using the Report Wizard

Before You Begin
The My Inventory Reporting database is open, and no objects are currently open in the documents pane.

Scenario
You will create a report to facilitate printing out your weekly list of orders that need to be placed to your suppliers.

Use the **Report Wizard** to create a report.

a) Select **Create→Reports→Report Wizard**.

b) In the **Tables/Queries** drop-down list, select **Query: qryReorderNow** and observe that fields from qryReorderNow are listed in the **Available Fields** list box.

c) Double-click each of the following field names to move them from **Available Fields** to **Selected Fields**:

- SupplierID
- ProductCode
- ItemDescription
- OrderQty
- OurUnitCost
- OrderCost
- Company

d) Observe that the company's address is not available in the **Available Fields** list. It was not included in the qryReorderNow query.

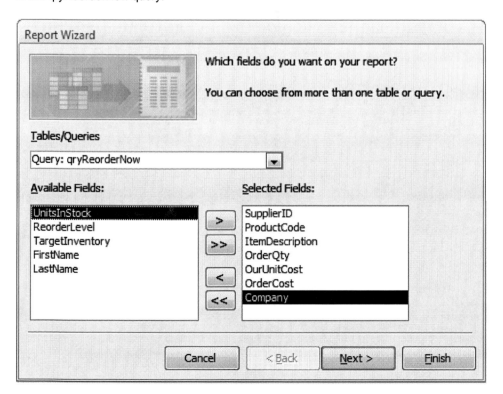

e) In the **Tables/Queries** drop-down list, select **Table: tblSuppliers** and observe that fields from tblSuppliers are listed in the **Available Fields** list box.

f) Double-click each of the following field names to move them from **Available Fields** to **Selected Fields**:
- ContactPhone
- ContactEmail
- Address
- City
- StateProvince
- Country
- PostalCode

g) Select **Next**.

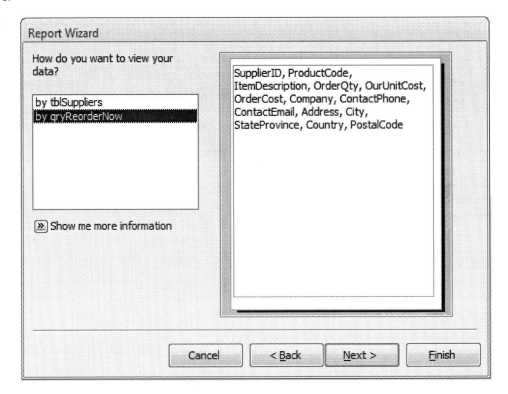

h) Select **Next** to accept the default view by qryReorderNow.

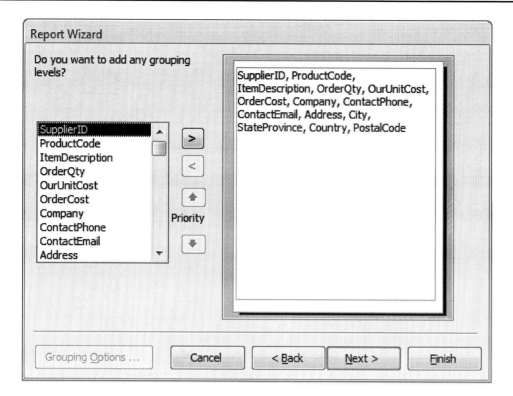

i) Select **Next** to accept the default grouping.
j) In the **1** drop-down list, select **SupplierID** and select **Next**.

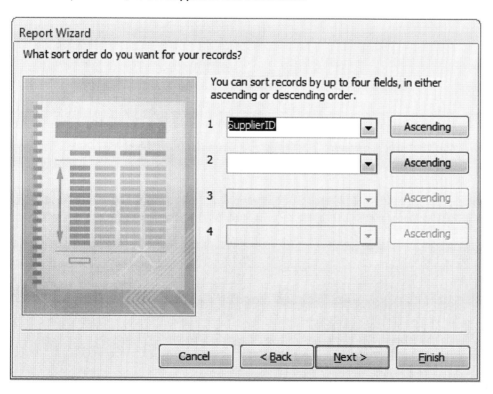

k) Verify that **Tabular** and **Portrait** are selected, and select **Next**.

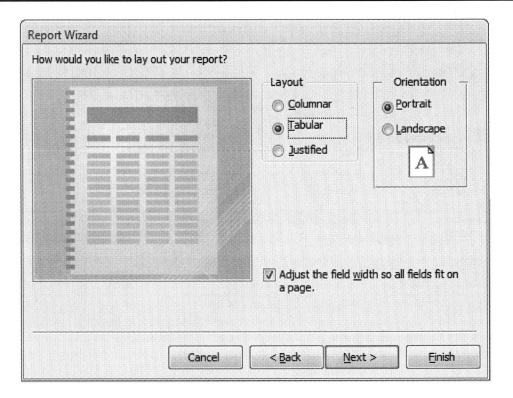

l) Change the report title to *rptListOfOrders* and select **Finish**.

m) Observe that the report is shown in a tabular format. Columns have been truncated at the page's right margin, so some layout adjustments are needed.

n) Close the report and save the database.

TOPIC B

Add Controls to a Report

The various tools you can use to generate a report often are able to do most or all of the creation of controls and layout for you. However, there are times when you will need to add controls manually.

Report Sections

The **Report Design View** is similar to the **Form Design View**. It provides bands for various sections of the report, including the report header, page header, group header, detail, group footer, page footer, and report footer. The **Detail** section is repeated for each record. Place information that should appear at the beginning and end of the report in the report header and footer. Place information that should appear on every page of the report in the page header and footer. Finally, place information that should appear for each group of data (if your report is organized by group) in the group header and footer.

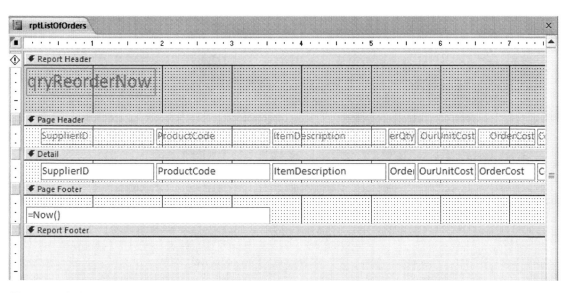

Figure 5–2: Sections in a report.

Control	Description
Text Box	Used to display values retrieved from tables and queries.
Label	Used to display headings and descriptive text.
Hyperlink	Used to display links to websites.
Combo Box	Used to allow users to select a value from a list or enter a value.
List Box	Used to allow users to select from a list of values.

Control Properties

Use the **Property Sheet** to set control properties. The **Property Sheet** organizes properties within tabs to make them easier to find. Tabs include **Format**, **Data**, **Event**, **Other**, and **All**.

Access the Checklist tile on your LogicalCHOICE course screen for reference information and job aids on How to Edit Controls in a Report

ACTIVITY 5-3
Adjusting Report Control Layout

Data Files

C:\091001Data\Generating Reports\Inventory Reporting 2.accdb (not to be opened until partway through the activity)

Before You Begin

The My Inventory Reporting database is open, and no objects are currently open in the documents pane.

Scenario

You are working toward producing the report layout shown here. In this activity, you will adjust the layout of controls in rptListOfOrders to better use the available space, as in the completed report.

Figure 5-3: The completed report.

1. Preview the current report layout.
   a) In the navigation pane, right-click **rptListOfOrders** tab and select **Print Preview**.
   b) Observe that the report does not fit completely on one page's width.

2. Move and resize the fields.
   a) Right-click the **rptListOfOrders** tab and select **Design View**. To enable each record to display across several rows, you will need to make the **Detail** band taller.
   b) Point at the top edge of the **Page Footer** section header. The mouse pointer becomes a double arrow.
   c) Drag the **Page Footer** section header down to create room to arrange fields in multiple rows.

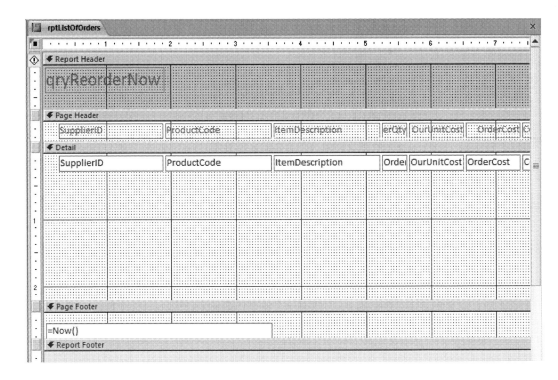

 Note: You do not have to set the height perfectly on the first attempt. You can always re-adjust the height later, after you have rearranged the text boxes.

d) Select the **Company** text box to select it. Point at one of the edges of the **Company** text box until you get a four-headed "move" arrow. Drag the **Company** text box into its new position below the **ProductCode** text box.

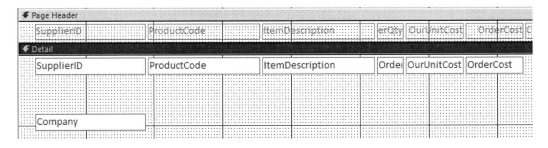

 Note: When you move **Company**, leave room above it for a label.

e) Make sure that the **Company** text box is still selected. Position the mouse pointer over the right edge of the **Company** text box where the mouse pointer becomes a resize arrow as shown.

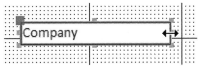

f) Drag to resize the **Company** text box as shown.

◀ Page Header					
SupplierID	ProductCode	ItemDescription	erQty	OurUnitCost	OrderCost
◀ Detail					
SupplierID	ProductCode	ItemDescription	Orde	OurUnitCost	OrderCost
Company					

 Note: As you perform this step, you may need to use the horizontal scroll bar to see the other text boxes.

 Note: To make fine adjustments, you may find it easier to use the keyboard than the mouse. Press the arrow keys to move the selected field or label. Hold the **Shift** key while pressing the arrow keys to change the width or height of the selected field or label.

g) Drag to move the label for **Company** from the **Page Header** band to the area above **Company**. Moving the label into the **Detail** area will cause it to repeat for every record in the report.

h) Save the database.

3. Open a more completed version of the report layout.

a) Close **My Inventory Reporting**.

b) Open the C:\091001Data\Generating Reports\Inventory Reporting 2.accdb database. Select **Enable Content** if you are prompted.

c) Save the database in C:\091001Data\Generating Reports as **My Inventory Reporting 2** and select **Enable Content** if you are prompted.

d) View rptListOfOrders in **Design View**. All of the fields and labels have been arranged in the **Detail** band using the same steps you used to move the **Company** field and label.

TOPIC C

Enhance the Appearance of a Report

Access provides numerous options to enhance the appearance of a report. For example, you can apply color themes and font styles, and add graphics to any band in a report design.

Galleries

A *gallery* provides a collection of layout elements or appearance settings that you can apply to a report or other database elements. The **Themes** gallery, for example, provides of style options (a combination of color schemes and fonts) that you can apply to a report.

Themes

Access provides various design themes that you can apply to forms and reports. To apply the theme, you open your form or report and select the **Themes** drop-down arrow in the **Design** tab. As you hover the mouse pointer over each theme, you can preview its effect on your design. Click the theme to select and apply it. The feature that enables you to preview the effect before you apply it is called *Live Preview*.

 Access the Checklist tile on your LogicalCHOICE course screen for reference information and job aids on How to Enhance the Appearance of a Report

ACTIVITY 5-4
Enhancing the Appearance of a Report

Before You Begin

The My Inventory Reporting 2 database is open and rptListOfOrders is displayed in the **Design** view.

Scenario

You will apply some final touches to your rptListOfOrders report, including changing the color theme and adding a graphic element.

---

1. Apply a theme to the report.
    a) Open rptListOfOrders in **Layout** view.
    b) In the **Design→Themes** group, select the **Themes** drop-down arrow. This gallery displays various graphic themes that you can apply to the report.
    c) Point at various themes in the gallery, and observe that a live preview of the theme is shown in the report. The themes are sorted alphabetically and the name of each theme appears in tooltip text as you point at the theme.

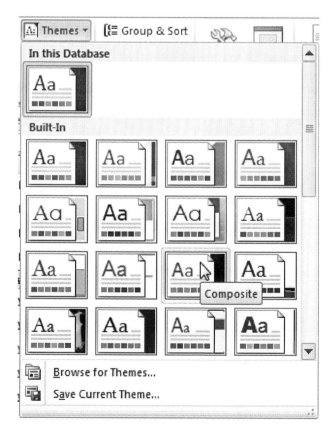

    d) Select the **Composite** theme to apply it to the report.

2. In the **Design→Themes** group, observe the buttons for the **Colors** and **Fonts** galleries. You can apply the colors and fonts from each theme separately. You could apply the colors from one theme and the fonts from another.

---

3. Add an image to the report.
   a) Display rptListOfOrders in **Design** view.
   b) Select **Design→Controls→Insert Image** and select **Browse**.
   c) Navigate to the folder C:\091001Data\Generating Reports, select **ww_logo.png**, and select **OK**. The mouse pointer becomes an **Image** icon.
   d) In the **Report Header** section, click just to the right of the **rptListOfOrders** title to place the image.
   e) Drag the image and the title caption to rearrange them as shown.

   f) Select the **rptListOfOrders** label. Then double-click in the label to select it for editing. Type *Order List*

   g) Right-click in the gray background of the header section.
   h) Select **Fill/Back Color**.
   i) Select the color white.

   j) Right-click the **rptListOfOrders** tab and select **Print Preview**.

4. Save the database.

TOPIC D

Prepare a Report for Print

When you print a report, you may find that the report contains too much information to fit within a page. Just a small amount of overlap into the page margin can cause odd page breaks when you print. It is often necessary to adjust page setup and layout options when you first set up a report for printing.

Page Setup Options

The **Page Setup** tab provides options that you can use to customize page properties before you print a report.

Option	Enables You To
Size	Select the paper size of the printed report.
Margins	Set the print margins to **Normal**, **Wide**, or **Narrow**.
Show Margins	Preview margin breaks.
Print Data Only	Print a report without column headers.
Portrait	Print a report using vertical paper orientation.
Landscape	Print a report using horizontal paper orientation.
Columns	Print a report in multiple columns.
Page Setup	Open the **Page Setup** dialog box.

The Print Preview Tab

The **Print Preview** tab provides various options to preview a report as it will appear when printed, before you actually print it.

Group	Description
Print	Provides a **Print** button that you can select to send the report to the printer.
Page Size	Includes various options related to paper size, page margins, and the **Print Data Only** option.
Page Layout	Includes options to change print orientation and column settings, and display the **Page Setup** dialog box.
Zoom	Provides options to change the magnification and number of pages shown at one time in **Print Preview** mode.
Data	Includes commands to export a report to the PDF and various other file formats.
Close Preview	Includes a button to exit **Print Preview** mode.

 Access the Checklist tile on your LogicalCHOICE course screen for reference information and job aids on **How to Prepare a Report for Print**

ACTIVITY 5-5
Preparing a Report for Print

Before You Begin

The My Inventory Reporting 2 database is open and rptListOfOrders is displayed in **Print Preview** view.

Scenario

Your report is just about ready to print. You will preview it and make any final adjustments that are necessary before printing.

Ensure that all of the controls fit within the page boundaries.

a) In the **Record** navigation bar, select the **Next Page** button.
b) Observe that a blank page 2 appears.
c) View several more pages and observe that there is a problem with page breaks.
d) Display rptListOfOrders in **Layout** view.
e) Observe no page content appears to spill across the page breaks, shown as dotted lines. Scroll to the left and right if your screen does not show the full page width.
f) Select **Format→Selection → Select All**. With all of the controls selected, you can see that **ItemDescription** overlaps the page breaks.
g) Click in an area of the report that contains no control to deselect the controls.

> **Note:** If you have multiple controls selected, when you drag to resize, you will resize all of the selected controls together.

h) Select the **ItemDescription** text field to select it.
i) Drag the right edge of the **ItemDescription** text field to the left until it fits within page boundaries.

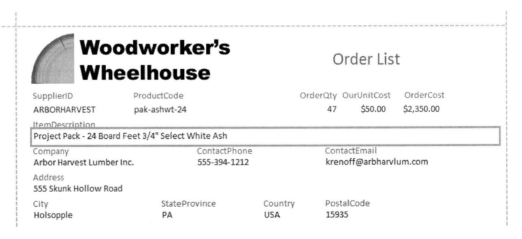

j) Display rptListOfOrders in **Print Preview**.
k) Use the **Record** navigation bar to navigate to page 2.
l) Observe the pagination problem has been resolved.
m) Save and close the database.

Summary

In this lesson, you learned how to create a report, add controls and change the report's layout, apply themes and layout options, and prepare it for print.

What sorts of reports will you need to produce?

You can print a datasheet. Why would you go to the additional effort to produce a report layout?

 Note: Check your LogicalCHOICE Course screen for opportunities to interact with your classmates, peers, and the larger LogicalCHOICE online community about the topics covered in this course or other topics you are interested in. From the Course screen you can also access available resources for a more continuous learning experience.

 Note: Access the LearnTO **Apply Conditional Row Formatting to a Report** presentation from the **LearnTO** tile on the LogicalCHOICE Course screen.

6 | Customizing the Access Environment

Lesson Time: 30 minutes

Lesson Objectives

In this lesson, you will customize the Access environment. You will:

*   Set configuration options in the **Access Options** dialog box.

Lesson Introduction

Access provides numerous options to enable you to customize the Microsoft® Office Access® 2010 application environment to meet your specific needs. In this lesson, you will explore the scope of options available in the **Access Options** dialog box, and will identify what configuration options would be appropriate to change in various situations.

TOPIC A

The Access Options Dialog Box

The **Access Options** dialog box provides a variety of configuration settings that enable you to customize database behavior and the Access user interface to meet your needs.

Access Options

Use the **Access Options** dialog box to customize and configure your installation of Access. Customization categories include **General, Current Database, Datasheet, Object Designers, Proofing, Language, Client Settings, Customize Ribbon, Quick Access Toolbar, Add-ins,** and **Trust Center**.

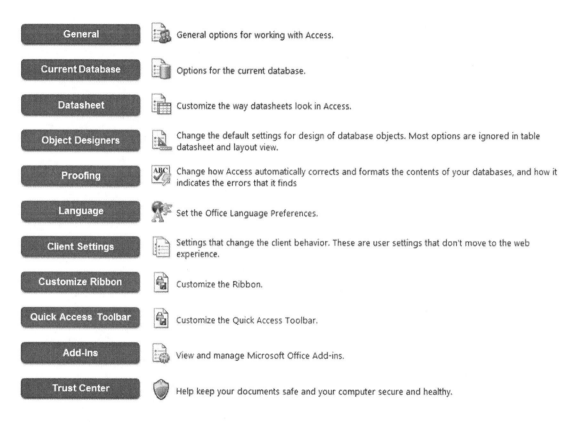

Figure 6-1: The Access Options dialog box.

 Access the Checklist tile on your LogicalCHOICE course screen for reference information and job aids on How to Set Access Options

ACTIVITY 6-1
Setting Access Options

Data Files

C:\091001Data\Customizing the Access Environment\Inventory Database.accdb

Scenario

In this activity, you will explore Access configuration options.

---

1. Open a database.
   a) In Access, select **File→Open** to display the **Open** dialog box.
   b) Open the C:\091001Data\Customizing the Access Environment\Inventory Database.accdb database. Select **Enable Content** if you are prompted.

2. Examine the scope of settings available in **Access Options**.
   a) Select **File→Options**. The **Access Options** dialog box is shown.
   b) Select each button in the left pane to view various options in the right pane. As you select each button, observe the summary description shown in the top of the right pane and scroll the right pane to view the scope of the settings available in each pane.

3. Find settings for the following options.

   Some users in your organization are still using Access 2003, so you want the default file format for new blank databases to be Access 2003.

4. You have a large high-resolution display monitor, and you want datasheets to display in a larger default font.

5. On a daily basis, you export data from various databases to PDF files, which you then post on a website. To save time, you want to add a shortcut to the Quick Access Toolbar to publish to a PDF.

6. Your company develops databases for government and military projects, and many uppercase acronyms are used. You want to take advantage of Office's proofing features, but you don't want the spelling checker to flag every acronym as a misspelling.

7. Your organization shares a database that is stored in a secure location on your network. You want to configure your installation of Access to enable advanced features only for databases opened from that Trusted Location.

8. Customize the **Quick Access Toolbar**.
   a) Select the **Quick Access Toolbar** tab to show the **Customize the Quick Access Toolbar** page.

b) In the **Choose commands from** drop-down list, select **All Commands.**.

c) In the list box beneath the **Choose commands from** drop-down list, select **Find** and select **Add > >** to add the **Find** command to the **Quick Access Toolbar**.

d) Select **OK**. The **Find** command has been added to the **Quick Access Toolbar**. (It will be dimmed if you do not have a table or query result open.) You can add any ribbon command to the **Quick Access Toolbar**, including some commands that are not displayed in the **Quick Access Toolbar**.

e) Exit Access.

Summary

In this lesson, you learned about configuration options that are available in the **Access Options** dialog box, and you added an icon to the **Quick Access Toolbar.**

What sort of configuration options do you think you will you use?

Are some locations safer to set as a trusted location than others?

 Note: Check your LogicalCHOICE Course screen for opportunities to interact with your classmates, peers, and the larger LogicalCHOICE online community about the topics covered in this course or other topics you are interested in. From the Course screen you can also access available resources for a more continuous learning experience.

Course Follow-Up

Congratulations! You have completed the *Microsoft® Office Access® 2010: Part 1* course. You have successfully created an Access database, including tables, forms, queries, and reports. With this knowledge, you will be able to effectively organize, manage, and analyze large amounts of data.

What's Next?

Microsoft® Office Access® 2010: Part 2 is the next course in this series. In that course, you will delve into database design; structure databases to optimize for efficiency, performance, and to maintain data integrity; share data between Access and other applications; and create advanced reports and forms.

You are encouraged to explore Access further by actively participating in any of the social media forums set up by your instructor or training administrator through the **Social Media** tile on the LogicalCHOICE Course screen.

Microsoft Office Access 2010 Exam 77-885

Selected Logical Operations courseware addresses Microsoft Office Specialist (MOS) certification skills for Microsoft Office 2010. The following table indicates where Access 2010 skills that are tested on Exam 77-885 are covered in the Logical Operations Microsoft Office Access 2010 series of courses.

Objective Domain	Covered In
1. Managing the Access Environment	
1.1. Create and Manage a Database	
1.1.1. Use Save Object As	Part 1, Topic 1-B
1.1.2. Use Open	Part 1, Topic 1-A
1.1.3. Use Save and Publish	Part 1, Topic 1-B
1.1.4. Use Compact & Repair Database	Part 3
1.1.5. Use Encrypt with Password Commands	Part 3
1.1.6. Create a Database from a Template	Part 1, Topic 1-B
1.1.7. Set Access Options	Part 1, Topic 6-A
1.2. Configure the Navigation Pane	
1.2.1. Rename Objects	Part 1, Topics 1-B, 5-B
1.2.2. Delete Objects	Part 1, Topics 1-A, 2-A
1.2.3. Set Navigation Options	Part 3
1.3. Apply Application Parts	
1.3.1. Use Blank Forms	Part 1, Topic 1-B; Part 3
1.3.2. Use Quick Start	Part 3
1.3.3. Use User Templates	Part 3
2. Building Tables	
2.1. Create Tables	
2.1.1. Create Tables in Design View	Part 1, Topic 1-B
2.2. Create and Modify Fields	
2.2.1. Insert a Field	Part 1, Topic 4-D
2.2.2. Delete a Field	Part 1, Topic 1-B

Objective Domain	Covered In
2.2.3. Rename a Field	Part 1, Topic 1-B
2.2.4. Hide or Unhide Fields	Part 1, Topic 1-B
2.2.5. Freeze or Unfreeze Fields	Part 1, Topic 2-B
2.2.6. Modify Data Types	Part 1, Topic 1-B
2.2.7. Modify the Field Description	Part 2
2.2.8. Modify Field Properties	Part 1, Topic 2-C
2.3. Sort and Filter Records	
2.1.3. Use Find	Part 1, Topic 2-B
2.3.2. Use Sort	Part 1, Topic 2-B
2.3.3. Use Filter Commands	Part 1, Topic 2-B
2.4. Set Relationships	
2.4.1. Define Primary Keys	Part 1, Topic 1-B; Part 2
2.4.2. Use Primary Keys to Create Relationships	Part 1, Topic 2-C; Part 2
2.4.3. Edit Relationships	Part 2
2.5. Import Data from a Single Data File	
2.5.1. Import Source Data Into a New Table	Part 2
2.5.2. Append Records to an Existing Table	Part 2
2.5.3. Import Data as a linked table	Part 2
3. Building Forms	
3.1.1. Use the Form Wizard	Part 1, Topic 1-B
3.1.2. Create a Blank Form	Part 1, Topic 1-B
3.1.3. Use Form Design Tools	Part 1, Topic 1-B
3.1.4. Create Navigation forms	Part 3
3.2. Apply Form Design Options	
3.2.1. Apply a Theme	Part 1, Topic 5-C
3.2.2. Add Bound Controls	Part 3
3.2.2.1. Text Box	Part 1, Topics 1-A, 1-C
3.2.2.2. Drop Down	Part 1, Topic 2-C
3.2.3. Format Header/Footer	Part 1, Topic 5-B
3.2.4. View Code	Part 3
3.2.5. Convert Macros to Visual Basic	Part 3
3.2.6. View Property Sheet	Part 1, Topic 2-C
3.2.7. Add Existing Fields	Part 1, Topic 1-B
3.3. Apply Form Arrange options	
3.3.1. Use the Table functions	Part 2
3.3.1.1. Insert	Part 2

Objective Domain	Covered In
3.3.1.2. Merge	Part 2
3.3.1.3. Split	Part 2
3.3.2. Move table	Part 2
3.3.3. Reposition / Format controls	Part 2
3.3.3.1. Anchor	Part 3
3.3.3.2. Padding	Part 2
3.3.3.3. Margins	Part 2
3.4. Apply Form Format Options	
3.4.1. Reformat Font in Form	Part 3
3.4.2. Apply Background Image to Form	Part 3
3.4.3. Apply Quick Styles to Controls in Form	Part 3
3.4.4. Apply Conditional Formatting in Form	Part 3
4. Creating and Managing Queries	
4.1. Construct Queries	
4.1.1. Create Select Query	Part 1, Topic 3-B
4.1.2. Create Make Table Query	Part 1, Topic 4-B
4.1.3. Create Append Query	Part 1, Topic 4-B
4.1.4. Create Crosstab Query	Part 1, Topic 4-B
4.2. Manage Source Tables and Relationships	Part 1, Topic 3-A; Part 2
4.2.1. Use the Show Table Command	Part 1, Topic 3-A; Part 2
4.2.2. Use Remove Table Command	Part 1, Topic 3-A; Part 2
4.2.3. Create Ad Hoc Relationships	Part 1, Topic 2-C; Part 2
4.3. Manipulate Fields	
4.3.1. Add Field	Part 1, Topic 3-A
4.3.2. Remove Field	Part 1, Topic 3-A
4.3.3. Rearrange Fields	Part 1, Topic 3-B
4.3.4. Use Sort and Show Options	Part 1, Topic 3-B
4.4. Calculate Totals	
4.4.1. Use the Total Row	Part 1, Topic 2-A
4.4.2. Use Group By	Part 1, Topic 2-A
4.5. Generate Calculated Fields	
4.5.1. Perform Calculations	Part 1, Topic 3-C
4.5.2. Use the Zoom Box	Part 1, Topic 3-B
4.5.3. Use Expression Builder	Part 1, Topic 3-C
5. Designing Reports	
5.1. Create Reports	

Objective Domain	Covered In
5.1.1. Create a Blank Report	Part 1, Topic 5-A
5.1.2. Use Report Design Tools	Part 1, Topic 5-B
5.1.3. Use the Report Wizard	Part 1, Topic 5-A
5.2. Apply Report Design Options	
5.2.1. Apply a Theme	Part 1, Topic 5-C
5.2.2. Add Calculated Controls	Part 2
5.2.2.1. Total Report Records	Part 2
5.2.2.2. Group Report Records	Part 2
5.2.3. Add Bound/Unbound Controls	Part 2
5.2.3.1. Text Box	Part 1, Topic 5-B
5.2.3.2. Hyperlink	Part 2
5.2.3.3. Drop Down	Part 2
5.2.3.4. Graph	Part 2
5.2.3.5. Insert Page Break	Part 2
5.2.4. Header/Footer	Part 1, Topic 5-B
5.2.4.1. Insert Page Number	Part 2
5.2.4.2. Insert Logo	Part 1, Topic 5-C
5.2.5. Reorder Tab Function	Part 2
5.3. Apply Report Arrange Options	
5.3.1. Use the Table Functions	Part 2
5.3.1.1. Insert	Part 2
5.3.1.2. Merge	Part 2
5.3.1.3. Split	Part 2
5.3.2. Move Table	Part 2
5.3.3. Reposition/Format Records	Part 2
5.3.3.1. Padding	Part 2
5.3.3.2. Margins	Part 2
5.3.4. Align Report Outputs to Grid	Part 2
5.4. Apply Report Format Options	
5.4.1. Rename Label in a Report	Part 1, Topic 5-C
5.4.2. Apply Background Image to Report	Part 2
5.4.3. Change Shape in Report	Part 2
5.4.4. Apply Conditional Formatting in Report	Part 1, Summary, LearnTO
5.5. Apply Report Page Setup Options	
5.5.1. Change Page Size	Part 2
5.5.2. Change Page Orientation	Part 2

Objective Domain	Covered In
5.6. Sort and Filter Records for Reporting	
5.6.1. Use the Find Command	Part 1, Topic 2-B
5.6.2. Use Sort Command	Part 1, Topic 2-B
5.6.3. Use Filter Commands	Part 1, Topic 2-B
5.6.4. Use View Types	Part 1, Topic 5-A

B | Microsoft Access 2010 Common Keyboard Shortcuts

The follow table lists common keyboard shortcuts you can use in Access 2010.

Function	Shortcut
Open a new database	Ctrl + N
Open an existing database	Ctrl + O
Open the **Print** dialog box	Ctrl + P
Open the **Find** tab	Ctrl + F
Copy the selected contents	Ctrl + C
Cut the selected contents	Ctrl + X
Paste the selected content	Ctrl + V
Undo typing	Ctrl + Z
Cycle between open windows	Ctrl + F6
Check spelling	F7
Rename a selected object	F2
Show the access keys	F10
Switch to the next tab in a dialog box	Ctrl + Tab
Switch to the previous tab in a dialog box	Ctrl + Shift + Tab
Move to the beginning of an entry	Home
Move to the end of an entry	End
Toggle the property sheet tab	F4
Toggle the **Field List** pane	Alt + F8
Insert the current data	Ctrl + ;
Insert the current time	Ctrl + Shift + :
Add a new record	Ctrl + +
Delete the current record	Ctrl + -
Save changes to the current record	Shift + Enter

Lesson Labs

Lesson labs are provided for certain lessons as additional learning resources for this course. Lesson labs are developed for selected lessons within a course in cases when they seem most instructionally useful as well as technically feasible. In general, labs are supplemental, optional unguided practice and may or may not be performed as part of the classroom activities. Your instructor will consider setup requirements, classroom timing, and instructional needs to determine which labs are appropriate for you to perform, and at what point during the class. If you do not perform the labs in class, your instructor can tell you if you can perform them independently as self-study, and if there are any special setup requirements.

Lesson Lab 1-1
Creating an Access Database

Activity Time: 10 minutes

Data Files

C:\091001Data\Getting Started with Access\Create Practice.accdb

C:\091001Data\Getting Started with Access\Solution\Create Practice.accdb

Scenario

You have started creating your inventory management database for the Woodworker's Wheelhouse. You have already created the first table, which will hold inventory data. Your administrative assistant has entered data in that table, but more tables are needed. The next table you will create will hold contact information for each of your product suppliers. In this practice lab, you will add a table to a database, and you will populate the first record.

---

1. Open the database C:\091001Data\Getting Started with Access\Create Practice.accdb. Select **Enable Content** if you are prompted.

2. Save the database in C:\091001Data\Getting Started with Access as *My Create Practice.accdb* and select **Enable Content** if you are prompted.

3. View tblInventory. This version of the database contains a table tblInventory that has been populated with 50 records of data.

4. Create a new table. Add the fields below. Name the table tblSuppliers.

Field Name	Data Type
SupplierID	Text
FirstName	Text
LastName	Text
ContactPhone	Text
Company	Text
ContactEmail	Text
Address	Text
City	Text
StateProvince	Text
Country	Text
PostalCode	Text

5. In table tblSuppliers, enter the following record.

Field Name	Data Type
SupplierID	ARBORHARVEST
FirstName	James
LastName	Krenoff
ContactPhone	555-394-1212
Company	Arbor Harvest Lumber Inc.
ContactEmail	krenoff@arbharvlum.com
Address	555 Skunk Hollow Road
City	Holsopple
StateProvince	PA
Country	USA
PostalCode	15935

6. Save and close the database.

Lesson Lab 2-1
Working with Tables

Activity Time: 10 minutes

Data Files

C:\091001Data\Working with Table Data\Table Practice.accdb

C:\091001Data\Working with Table Data\Solution\Table Practice.accdb

Scenario

To minimize data entry errors when users select a department, you will change the **Dept** field to use a table lookup.

1. Open the database C:\091001Data\Working with Table Data\Table Practice.accdb. Select **Enable Content** if you are prompted.

2. Save the database in C:\091001Data\Working with Table Data as *My Table Practice.accdb* and select **Enable Content** if you are prompted.

3. Change the **Dept** field of frmInventory to be a combo box. Set its row source to provide a drop-down list of departments that are available in the tblDepartments table.

4. Close all open tabs, saving changes when you are prompted.

5. Establish a table relationship between the **Department** field of tblDepartments and the **Dept** field of tblInventory. Enforce referential integrity so only valid values are permitted in the **Dept** field.

6. Save the database.

7. To test your new lookup field, display frmInventory in **Form View**. Use the drop-down list to change the **Dept** for bathhw-2 from "Bathroom" to "Décor."

8. Close the database.

Lesson Lab 3-1
Queries

Activity Time: 10 minutes

Data Files

C:\091001Data\Querying a Database\Query Practice.accdb

C:\091001Data\Querying a Database\Solution\Query Practice.accdb

Scenario

You need to print inventory tags that you fasten to all of the storage racks in your showroom and warehouse. The tags each include the product code, storage location and rack number, and the name of the manufacturer. To produce a list of information you will need for all inventory, you will produce the query shown here.

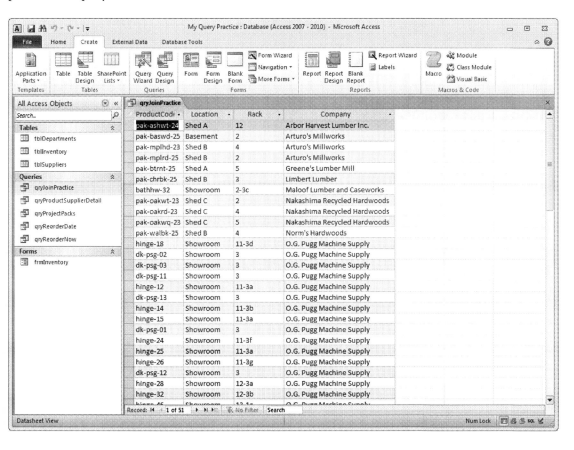

1. Open the database C:\091001Data\Querying a Database\Query Practice.accdb. Select **Enable Content** if you are prompted.

2. Save the database in C:\091001Data\Querying a Database as *My Query Practice.accdb* and select **Enable Content** if you are prompted.

3. Create a query that displays the following fields:

- tblInventory: *ProductCode*
- tblInventory: *Location*
- tblInventory: *Rack*
- tblSuppliers: *Company*

4. Configure the query to sort the results in **Ascending** order by **Company**.

5. Name the query *qryInventoryTags* and save the database.

6. Run the query and verify that it is producing the required results.

7. Close the database.

Lesson Lab 4-1
Advanced Queries

Activity Time: 10 minutes

Data Files

C:\091001Data\Creating Advanced Queries\Advanced Query Practice.accdb

C:\091001Data\Creating Advanced Queries\Solution\Advanced Query Practice.accdb

Scenario

So that you can quickly find the location of a product in your store, you want to create a query that will find text within the **ItemDescription** field and return any matches, along with the associated product codes and locations.

---

1. Open the database C:\091001Data\Creating Advanced Queries\Advanced Query Practice.accdb. Select **Enable Content** if you are prompted.

2. Save the database in C:\091001Data\Creating Advanced Queries as *My Advanced Query Practice.accdb* and select **Enable Content** if you are prompted.

3. Create a query that meets the following requirements:
    *   Returns the fields **ProductCode**, **ItemDescription**, **RetailPrice**, **Location**, and **Rack** from the tblInventory table.
    *   When the query runs, display the following prompt: *Search Item Description For*.
    *   Based on the value the user enters, the query will return a list of products whose **ItemDescription** contains the text that was entered. Text that appears anywhere within **ItemDescription** should be found.

4. Name the query *qryDescriptionSearch*.

5. Save the database.

6. Test the query to verify that it works correctly.

7. Close the database.

Lesson Lab 5–1
Reports

Activity Time: 10 minutes

Data Files

C:\091001Data\Generating Reports\Report Practice.accdb

C:\091001Data\Generating Reports\Solution\Report Practice.accdb

Scenario

You need to print out tags that can be cut and slipped into a clear envelope on the storage bins and racks in the Woodworker's Wheelhouse store. An example report is shown here.

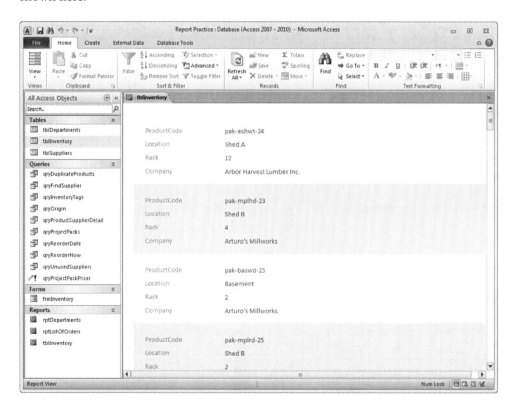

1. Open the database C:\091001Data\Generating Reports\Report Practice.accdb. Select **Enable Content** if you are prompted.

2. Save the database in C:\091001Data\Generating Reports as *My Report Practice.accdb* and select **Enable Content** if you are prompted.

3. Create a report named rptInventoryTags that shows all of the fields in qryInventoryTags. The report should produce tags that can be cut and slipped into a clear envelope on the storage bins and racks in the Woodworker's Wheelhouse store. Refer to the layout example provided with the scenario. Your layout does not need to match the example exactly.

4. Save the database.

5. Test your report layout, and verify that it meets the requirements described.

6. Close the database.

Solutions

ACTIVITY 1–1: Considering Potential Uses for Access

---

1. **Why did you decide to use Access?**

   A: Answers will vary.

2. **Considering the work you do, what sorts of tools or databases would you like to create in Access?**

   A: Answers will vary depending on individual needs.

3. **Regarding your response to the previous question, what data might you need to keep within such a database?**

   A: Answers will vary. To know what information needs to go into the database, it is helpful to know what information you want to get out of the database. Will it drive a monthly report? Will it help you track the status of certain tasks or products? Will it help you know where things are stored? Will it hold information you intend to publish? What you want the database to do for you will help determine what information you need within the database.

ACTIVITY 1–10: Getting Help in Access

---

3. If you have remote learners accessing through a web conference, be sure to keep them involved in this activity. For example, if your web conferencing system enables learners to easily share their desktops, you can have learners show what they have found in their search so that the entire class can view their findings. Remind learners that they can search locations other than Access Help by selecting All Access.
   What are the first three steps of a database design process?

   A: Answers may vary, depending on which article you find. For example, one Help article ("The Design Process") provides the following steps to designing a database: 1) Determine the purpose of your database, 2) Find and organize the information required, 3) Divide the information into tables, 4) Turn information items into columns, 5) Specify primary keys, 6) Set up the table relationships, 7) Refine your design, and 8) Apply the normalization rules.

ACTIVITY 2–7: Configuring a Form Lookup Field

---

7. After learners have had time to think about and jot down their answers to the following questions, have volunteers share their responses.
What is the benefit of establishing a lookup field?

A: A lookup field enables users to pick from a list of acceptable values.

8. **What is the benefit of establishing a table relationship and enforcing referential integrity?**

A: Referential integrity ensures that every value in one table is contained within the related field of another table. This is important for keeping the table relationship useful as a means of connecting the two tables.

ACTIVITY 3-3: Filtering a Query Using a Comparison Operator

---

2. Give learners time to consider and discuss this question. Those participating through web conferencing can post responses in the class chat/messaging system.
Which fields would enable you to determine which items need to be reordered?

A: UnitsInStock could be compared to ReorderLevel. If UnitsInStock is less than or equal to ReorderLevel, then it's time to place an order.

ACTIVITY 3-6: Performing Calculations in a Query

---

2. Give learners time to consider and discuss this question. Be sure to provide opportunity for remote learners to respond.
How might you determine how many of each item you need to order?

A: The **UnitsInStock** field shows how many items are currently in stock. The **ReorderLevel** field shows how few items should be in stock to trigger reordering. The **TargetInventory** field shows the number of items you should have in stock after replenishing your supply. Subtract **UnitsInStock** from **TargetInventory** to produce the replenish amount.

ACTIVITY 5-1: Creating Reports

---

3. Refer learners back to the table in the section Report Creation Tools. Involve remote learners by having learners post responses in the class chat/messaging system.
What approach would you use to quickly create a report that lists all of the fields from the tblInventory table?

A: The **Report** command (**Create→Reports→Report**) might be the most direct approach in this case. It quickly creates a report that uses all fields from the selected table or query.

ACTIVITY 6-1: Setting Access Options

---

3. If you have remote learners, involve them in the discussion by having them post responses in the class chat/messaging system.
Some users in your organization are still using Access 2003, so you want the default file format for new blank databases to be Access 2003.

A: In the **General** section, you would set **Default file format for Blank Database** to **Access 2002 - 2003**.

4. You have a large high-resolution display monitor, and you want datasheets to display in a larger default font.

    A: In the **Datasheet** section, in the **Default font** group, you would set the size to a larger value.

5. On a daily basis, you export data from various databases to PDF files, which you then post on a website. To save time, you want to add a shortcut to the Quick Access Toolbar to publish to a PDF.

    A: In the **Quick Access Toolbar** section, you would add **PDF or XPS** to the **Quick Access Toolbar**.

6. Your company develops databases for government and military projects, and many uppercase acronyms are used. You want to take advantage of Office's proofing features, but you don't want the spelling checker to flag every acronym as a misspelling.

    A: In the **Proofing** section, in the **When correcting spelling in Microsoft Office programs** group, you would make sure that **Ignore words in UPPERCASE** is checked.

7. Your organization shares a database that is stored in a secure location on your network. You want to configure your installation of Access to enable advanced features only for databases opened from that Trusted Location.

    A: In the **Trust Center** section, select the **Trust Center Settings** button to display the **Trust Center** dialog box. Select **Trusted Locations** to display the pane in which you can specify trusted locations.

Glossary

action query
A type of query that modifies data in records that meet search criteria.

append query
A type of action query that copies fields or records from one table to another.

arithmetic operators
A symbol or sign used to perform mathematical operations on field values.

calculated field
A field that displays values that are produced mathematically based on values in other fields.

comparison operators
A sign or symbol, or combination of signs and symbols, that compare values and produce a true, false, or null result based on the relationship between the values; include <, <=, >, >=, =, and <>.

crosstab query
A query that calculates and summarizes table data by category.

data
Qualitative or quantitative values that can be recorded in a database.

database
An organized collection of data. This term also refers to the file (such as an Access .accdb file) that stores a database.

delete query
A type of action query that deletes fields or records from a table.

expression
A combination of functions, field names, numbers, text, and operators that produces a result.

Expression Builder
An Access dialog box that supports a database developer in selecting database objects and building formulas used in queries and reports.

filtering
A database operation that shows only those records where values within a specified field meet required query criteria. For example, a filter may show all those records that include telephone numbers in the area code "555."

Find Duplicates Query
A type of query that finds records that contain duplicate field values within a table or query.

Find Unmatched Query
A type of query that finds records that exist in one record set but not the other, when comparing two tables or queries.

flat database
A database that contains a single table of data.

foreign key

A field that is linked to the primary key in another table. To establish such a link, the primary key and foreign key fields must have the same data type. Duplicate values can appear in foreign key fields, but unique values must exist in primary key fields.

gallery

An Access feature that displays a list of layout elements or appearance settings that you can apply to a report or other database elements.

information

In the context of database development, data that has been organized or transformed to produce a message or meaning.

knowledge

In the context of database development, data that has been organized or transformed to produce results that inform action.

like operator

An operator that is used within a query criterion to search for records based on a wildcard pattern.

Live Preview

An Access feature that applies style and theme changes immediately as you point at various style and theme commands in Access, so you can see the result of a style or theme change before you actually apply it.

logical operators

An established word used in an expression that evaluate values passed into them and produce a true or false result based on logic; include AND, OR, and NOT.

make table query

A type of action query that copies values from one or more existing tables or queries into another table.

multi-level sort

A type of sort that arranges records in order based on the values in more than one field.

parameter query

A type of query that enables a user to pass information into a query just before it runs.

PivotChart

A graphical display of PivotTable data.

PivotTable

A type of crosstab query that arranges data in a view that organizes data into a grid, with one category arranged across the top (columns) and another category arranged across the left side (rows). It provides a calculated value at the intersection of each column and row.

primary key

A field that is configured to require a unique value in each record. No two records in the table may have the same field value, and each record must contain a value in the primary key field. Because the field contains unique values, it can be used as a unique identifier for a record. Fields that are designated as a primary key are shown in **Design View** with a **Key** icon.

primary sort

A type of sort that is done last in a multi-level sort. It will have the most apparent effect on the resulting sort order, since it may shuffle the results of previous sorts.

Property Sheet

An Access window in which you can change the property values of the selected database object.

query criteria

Expressions that provide rules by which a query determines which records to display in its output. Criteria are written as mathematical or logical expressions that evaluation to true (a matching record, which will be displayed) or false (not a matching record, which will not be displayed).

Query Design

A view of a query that is optimized for performing query-defining tasks such as adding fields to the query, specifying sorts, adding criteria, and so forth.

Record navigation bar

Shown in datasheet and form views, a screen element that provides controls that you can use to navigate among records.

referential integrity

A database quality where every foreign key in every table has a link to a primary key in another table. Ensuring referential integrity prevents entry of invalid data.

relational database

A database that contains multiple tables of data that relate to each other through certain key fields.

Report Wizard

A dialog box that guides you through steps to create a report based on one or more tables or queries, enabling you to select which fields you want to include in the report. The wizard also provides options to group and sort data, and to customize the layout of reports.

Run Command

Available from the **Design** tab on the ribbon, a command that enables you to launch a query from **Design** view to see the results of the query.

secondary sort

A sort done before the primary sort in a multi-level sort. The secondary sort will have the less effect on the resulting sort order, since the primary sort may shuffle the results of the secondary sort when it runs. Use a secondary sort as a sub-sort. For example, if the primary sort is on the **Department** and the secondary sort is on the **ProductCode**, then groups of records that are all from the same **Department** will be sorted by **ProductCode**.

select query

A type of query that pulls a copy of one or more fields from one or more data sources based on selection criteria.

Simple Query Wizard

A dialog box that prompts you through steps to create a query. Advanced features can be applied in **Query Design** view after the wizard has finished creating the query.

sorting

A process that involves arranging items in alphanumeric order based on the values each record contains within the field on which the sort is applied.

table relationship

A link between two tables based on values in fields that share a common data type.

update query

A type of action query that performs an update operation on the values in records that meet specific query criteria. For example, an update query might apply a price discount to all products in the Tools department.

view

A portion of the interface provided in the **File** tab of the Access ribbon. It provides options related to file format and file management.

wildcard

Symbols that you can place in a query criterion to match records based on patterns, rather than requiring a literal character-by-character match.

Index

Z

Zoom dialog box *89*